AF539532

TAPPED
YET UNROOTED

POETIC WORD SLAUGHTER

BY

J.E. ROME

For permission requests, write to the publisher, addressed "Attention: Permissions Coordinator," at the address below.

Publish Your Purpose Press
141 Weston Street, #155
Hartford, CT, 06141

The opinions expressed by the Author are not necessarily those held by Publish Your Purpose Press.

Ordering Information: Quantity sales and special discounts are available on quantity purchases by corporations, associations, and others. For details, contact the publisher at orders@publishyourpurposepress.com.

Edited by: Cris Cruz
Cover design by: Cris Cruz
Typeset by: Medlar Publishing Solutions Pvt Ltd., India

Printed in the United States of America.
ISBN: 978-1-951591-07-6 (hardcover)
ISBN: 978-1-951591-06-9 (paperback)
ISBN: 978-1-951591-08-3 (ebook)

Library of Congress Control Number: 2020933507

First edition, May 2020

This book is dedicated to **YOU**.

YOU who felt forced to hide behind **SILENCE**.
YOU who witnessed your fair share of **VIOLENCE**.
YOU who were failed by ancestral **GUIDANCE**.
YOU who ponders permanently closed **EYELIDS**.

To those of **YOU** who were turned away, when
YOU finally found the courage to speak out,
by the person in which **YOU** had **CONFIDED**.

YOU that've cut, binged, purged, regurged,
repeated, 'n submerged, all of your self—worth
in the belief that you were ultimately birthed
jus' to remain regretfully quiet—**LIKE "I" DID** . . .

"HE" did . . .
"THEY" did . . .
"WE" did!

We're **ALL** in this **TOGETHER**!

To:
YOU who's ever said,
or felt, that y'boy was
truly destined towards
somethin' **G R E A T** . . .

My sincerest apologies
for showin' up so late.

Never meant t'make you wait.
I'll forever appreciate the faith.

—rome

Without further ado . . .
IT'S TIME YOU GET TAPPED!

Artist: Jason Boucher

CONTENTS

WIENER, WINNER

This the start of his existence.
They chose the path of least resistance.
He's not a seed of persistence.
He's a one-hit wonder.
A MISTAKE . . . that went the distance.
He could have been erased within an instance.
Of which, they'd remind him with consistence.
So it begins . . .

"TAKE YOUR MARKS!"

He's on the startin' blocks.
It's time to take his stance.
This is high-stakes swimmin'.
In a race, to the eggs . . .
you only get ONE chance.

At the sound of the gun, forward he'd lunge.
Into the pool of hope, he catches his first glance . . .
at the finish line, of happenstance.
Wigglin' his way, without the use of any hands.

He's the prodigal son.

YESSS!
HE'S THE SPERM THAT WON!

If he had a pair of feet,
he'd do a victory dance.

Nothin' bothers him more,
than when they go into their rants
about how they'd given up their life,
for him, under "grave circumstance."

They'd become pregnant,
stemmin' from a rendezvous
lackin' romance.
Damn,
their siblin' is gonna be pissed,
when they find out about this prance.

I think it's pretty safe to bet
that allowin' a horizontal dance,
with their spouse, wasn't in the plans.

Yet, this is how he entered the fam—
On a wham-bam, "thank you!"
of a siblin' exchange program.

They'll always remind him
that he was unplanned.
But there's still **ONE** thing that,
to this day, he doesn't fully understand.

How the fuck is he to blame,
because **THEY**
couldn't keep **IT**
in **THEIR** pants!?

BRACE YOURSELF—PT. I

I'm writin' away
from my problems.

I know this doesn't,
necessarily, solve 'em.

It's merely the quickest Band-aid,

I could find—to abruptly resolve 'em . . .

And that's just fine—by me,
if I'm bein' openly candid.

I've come to the sad realization that
the family that one builds
is stronger than the family
that one has been handed.

As we aquire the ones
that appreciate us,
'n let go of all those
that have taken us
for granted . . .

So, when I write away
from all of my problems,
I gladly leave 'em all—behind, stranded.

And never again will I ask myself,

"Why me!?"

You see . . .
When I envision a family tree . . .
I think of every branch
as a memory in time.

The substance of
all relationships lies
within the branches
that most families
continuously climb.

Some of the branches

are strong.
Over-filled with leaves
of love,
happiness,
‘n rewards.

While others are weak,
empty,
easily bendable,
‘n snap upon the force
of the trials
‘n tribulations
of life . . .

As “human nature” runs its course.

Sometimes we fall
‘n hit every branch
down along the way.

In these situations,

a weak family gives up
on one another.
On that ground
is where they choose
their relationships remain.

A strong family, however,
will pick each other back up,
‘n begin to climb again.
Not allowin’ setbacks
to supersede each gain.

Then, there’s his . . .

the ones that turn their backs,
'n disown each other,
at the drop of a dime.

Not t'be outdone
are those that abuse substances,
their seeds,
one another,
'n commit many a felonious crime.

Pedophilic behavior?

Yeah,
it's time to make change.
So, let's drop a metaphorical freakin' dime.

Sad, but TRUE,
these are but a select few
of the UNFORGIVABLE thoughts
that have REALLY SCREWED WITH HIS MIND!

He's often baffled, himself,
by the g'damn lowlifes
that continuously cover this
metaphorical tree in grime.

That shit happens,
all the fuckin' time!

Oh,
I guess I should probably
forewarn you . . .

Before you continue to read.
I'm goin' to curse—A LOT!
Which isn't necessarily like me.

I mean,
it's been known to happen.
But never has it occurred,
within my poetry.

Although, I promise,
you'll still know it's me.

As I'ma hold nothin' back,
'n let the story grow
ridiculously free.

Startin' from the roots.
Endin' wherever the portraits,
that hang from the branches,
of this dysfunctional tree—may lead.
Or should I say wind up!?

Eh . . . fuck it.
Whatever's meant t'be, you'll read.

TAPPED YET UNROOTED—PT. II

Tapped, yet unrooted . . .
is his family tree.

A metaphor of sorts,
designed to mislead.

It's the wrong one to bark up,
if you're ever in dire need.

Hell . . .
They can barely help themselves.

Consumed, by selfishness
'n greed.

Troubled is the soil,
that fermented the seeds.
The majority have grown up,
'n blossomed,
into beautiful leaves.

While others remain weathered,
like the alcoholics
that would breed.
Not to mention those
that pop pills,
shoot up,
'n smoke—from the purplish weeds.

While most of the morals
have sprouted intact . . .
others still remain
deeply buried.

All covered in manure . . .
feces . . .
debris . . .

Okay, SHIT!

They're covered in shit.
To which their odors are,
mockingly, complimentary.
You can usually smell the bullshit,
without ever havin'
visited previously
with their tree.

Which is why
we've got to assign
everyone a new HIGHLY
top-secret—metaphoric—identity.

We can't have you
all kinds of confused,
over every other
"he," "she," "I," 'n "we."

Which, for the most part,
is what you will see.

Since names are forbidden.
Oh, woe is me.

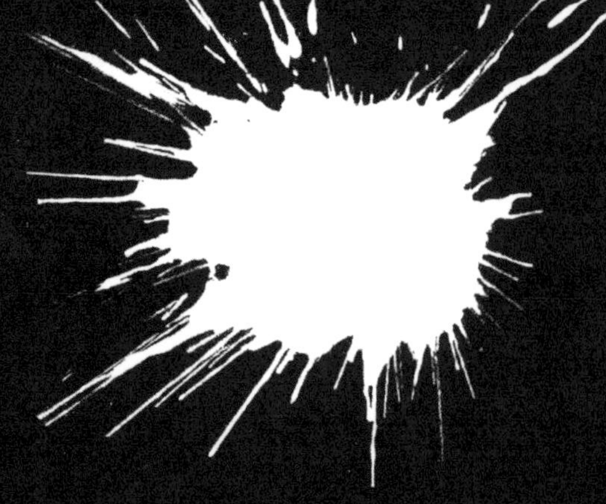

While we tell you all
about their upbringin',
in this catty, chatty,
"sue happy" tree.

Speakin' of bullshit,
allow us to start
with the leaves . . .

You could refer to them as "adults."
Against their own, often bitter, beliefs.
Aunts, uncles, parents, grandparents,
friends, friends of friends, some cousins,
friends they were made to call "aunt"/"uncle," etc.
(I know—it's like, "Jeez!")

But for argument's sake,
let's just call them "leaves."

We often question whether they've

fully grown up . . .
with all of their senseless quarrels,
'n immature beefs.

Or if some of them ever will . . .

The kids . . .
we'll call them seeds.
Cousins, siblings, 'n children.
Pretty simplistic, indeed.

Oh,
for clarity's sake,
we may even throw in some
apples 'n nuts.

Every tree's got 'em.
You know . . .
the crazies 'n such.

Then there's those that spoil, etc.
You'll quickly get the picture.
Call it a hunch.

Tapped, yet unrooted.
They're no Brady Bunch.

HEARD THIS BEFORE

People seem to think
that he's always had it made.

They have no clues
as to the fucked-up dues

which he's overly paid.

He's become a family recluse,
stemmed from years of abuse.
On his mind,
it's all heavily weighed.

Whenever we repeat a thought,
that's how heavily it's weighed.

Over, 'n over, in his head . . .
it's been redundantly replayed.

He never asked, for any of this.

He had no choice, in this journey,
about which he'll regrettably reminisce.

God's decision was made—pre-seed.
Bein' related to these people
is a fact that he's forced to concede.

It's a good thing for him,
that THEY were PRO-seed.

That side of the family didn't want THEM
to move forward—abortion? PROCEED!

He's been handed a life sentence.
Talk about a condemned Swede.

Although he's committed no crime,
He's doin' the time.
He will not be allowed
to roam around—carefree.

This is where he'll be forced to grow,
from head to toe.
Locked up—in captivity.

He's got the whole place to himself.
It's important to his health,
that there's plenty of fluids,
for him—to breathe.

Since the hostess takes care
of his womb 'n board
(which is more than he can currently afford),
he's growin' in there—rent-free.

Clear of any of the outside anarchy,
none of which does he want—or need.
He's got his own issues to resolve,
before they'll allow him to leave.

They've detected a hole in his heart—an abnormality.
Birthed into an incubator from the start—is the formality.

Yet,
he'll be a fighter, his entire existence . . .
WE PROMISE YOU—they're all gonna see.

CULINARY CHAOS

We don't understand
how the hell they made it
off of that branch
in one piece . . .
(let alone alive.)

Every day, for them,
was a struggle.
There was very little value
held on a seed's life.

How can they still
show their love to
those two leaves,
that have tried
to kill them . . .

not just once,
but at least
TWICE!?

This leaf's heart is as cold as ice.
The intent is that their seeds
pay the ultimate price.

The cake that was baked
is laced—with poisonin'.
Yet, it's not intended
for rats, nor mice.

This is a means to an end.
An inhumane, culinary device.

If that leaf was havin'
any second thoughts . . .
IT'S TOO LATE!
Someone's already creeped
into the fraudulent dessert,
'n snuck themselves a slice.
Now the leaf's position's
been fully compromised.

They're, straight up, caught in a panic.
Interrogatin' seed by seed.
But they can't determine
who's tellin' them
compound lies.

This leaf's become exceedingly frantic.

The home enemas,
that they've started administerin'
(to each seed) won't stop . . .
'til one of the seeds finally complies.

Or . . .

worst case scenario,
one, or more, of them dies . . .

The house is consumed,
by fear-induced cries.

Until they finally
get their breakthrough.

A confession,
through tear-filled eyes.

A blessin', in disguise.

'cause that would be
the last time
that this leaf tries
playin' Grim Reaper
with innocent lives.

SAY WHAT?

When it comes to firsts,
leaves are overwhelmingly proud
of everythin' that seeds do.

For example:
a seed's first words
are a heart-meltin', momentous virtue.

Whether it be "such 'n such" or "this 'n that,"
a speakin' baby is EXTREMELY cute.

His however . . .
oh, his.
His are the words that they wished
he'd chosen NOT to use.
Yes, we said "words."
Not one—but TWO.

His first exclamation, as an infant,
should've sparked up a clue.

That someday he'd pop off at the mouth.
Based upon all that he's seen,
from his own point of view.

Literally crawlin' under the radar,
while lookin' up—at all that they'd do.

He's the quietest witness to testify.
Takin' mental crib notes,
of all the ridiculousness that ensued.

But no one could've guessed,
that he'd verbally express THOSE feelings—this soon.

Overwhelmed by all the scandal 'n chaos.
This, we assume,
is the only explanation for the words
that he was prepared to spit.

After everythin' he's been exposed to,
it's all come down to this!

The first glorious words that rolled off his tongue's tip . . .
Were an over-resoundin'
(as if to say, "What the fuck did they birth him into")

"OH, SHIT!"

MISSIN' LEAF AD

What the fuck happened,
to finishin' what you're startin'!?

When he began plantin' seeds,
he put his entire heart in.

But this other motherfucker
blew off of the tree, for milk,
'n breezed back on the carton!

In doin' so,
you forever changed the lives,
of every one of the seeds,
that you played NO PART in.

It's far too late
to change the past.
You're not worth

them bogartin' (bullyin')

If you don't hear them fully, then . . .
they'll have to start shoutin'.

HOW COULD YOU TURN
YOUR BACK ON THEM?

AND THEM . . .

AND EVERYONE ELSE THAT,
SINCE, BEARS YOUR NAME.

THEY'VE WITNESSED THEIR
UNDER-DEVELOPMENTS.
IT'S A CRYIN'-FUCKIN'-SHAME!

IT FEELS LIKE THEY'RE POINTIN'
FINGERS—IN THE DARK,
'CAUSE YOU'LL NEVER
VISUALLY BE HERE
TO ACCEPT THE BLAME.

THEY WOULD CALL YOU OUT,
BUT COWARDS DON'T
DESERVE THE FAME

'N EVEN IF THEY DID,
WHAT'S THAT SHIT
GONNA CHANGE?

AT THE END OF THE DAY,
THERE'S ONLY ONE THING,
ABOUT YOU,
THAT WILL FINALLY STAY.

. . . that will finally frickin' STAY.

They still love you, unconditionally,
no matter what you do,
or didn't do.

No matter what you've said,
or didn't say.

Their love for you,
remains the same.

Their love for you,
will always stay.

Even if you passed away . . .

It's such a shame
that it had t'be
this way.

POTTY ROCKIN'

He's poppin' baby bottles, up in this bitch.
That's what happens,
when alcohol's no stranger—like this.

This was his bedtime anthem.
C'mon, throw your damn hands up!
This was his nightly cheer.

Jump up 'n down, in your crib!
Spit up all over your bibs!
This was his style of bedtime jeer.

TAPPED YET UNROOTED

Let's make some noise!
Clank together your toys!
It's time to scream out loud,
without any fear.

It's time to tear this mutha out!
All together, let's shout!

"I want juice!
I want milk!
I want *wala*!
I want BEER!"

Yes, you heard him loud.
Yes, you heard him clear.

"I want juice!
I want milk!
I want *wala*!
I want BEER!"

This was his bedtime anthem.
Wave all of your bottles, way up in the air!
We're each gon' drink more than our share!

The party's jumpin' off, in his crib.
The next boob that struts by, HE'S GOT DIBS!
Tonight his drinks might be on tap—by brassiere.

"I want juice!
I want milk!
I want *wala*!
I want BEER!"

We know we're makin' light of this thought.
These definitely aren't the words—from our seeds—

that we'd wanna hear.
I mean, we understand the want for juice, milk, or water.
But why the fuck, as an infant, was he callin' out for BEER!?
And . . . he's never had a sip of alcohol, in his life.
That's what we call irony . . . "HEAR, HEAR!"

He's poppin' baby bottles . . .

BEDTIME STRESS

It's THURSDAY, 10:47 PM,
'n he's goin' through
nightly, pre-dream, strife.

She's, hands down,
the scariest person
he's ever met—in his entire life.

The star of many nightmares.

The "Boogie Ma'am"
of his sleepless nights.

She's the epitome
of all his fears,
thrown together
in a hellish hand basket,
'n combined.

She's a walkin' scary movie.
She's his thoughts of horror—personified.

He's learned to sleep
with one eye open.

He's scared to death,
to close both eyes.

He's unsure whether
or not she's plottin'.

Tonight could lead
to their demise.

A double dose of anti-psycho,
is what the doctor should prescribe.

Better make that a triple.
One can't be too safe . . .

Get the vibe?

He wet the bed for years,
from fears
he can't (to this day) describe.

Maybe he'll attempt that later.

If he can muster up the words,
that he struggles so much to voice.

The cat 'o nine tails
is her weapon of choice.

She'd put a lashin'
on some asses.

God, help them boys . . .
'n girls.
Or whoever else
was 'bout to catch it.

If you pissed her off,
then you were catchin' lashes.

On the back.
On the legs.
'N everywhere—in between . . .
If you were on the spot.

We shit you not.

This bitch was fuckin' MEAN!

It's like he's trapped in a scary movie.

Replayin' scene,
after scene,
after scene.

'Cause to this very day,
from the casket in her grave,
she haunts him in his dreams.

sighs
Good night . . .

COCK FIGHT

At times it's tough
to reflect back on his seedhood
'n how some of their time
was spent.

The'yre back on the Boogie Ma'am's branch.
Where the fear wilts free—no rent.

TAPPED YET UNROOTED

Everyone's hangin' out,
while circled around, content.

It looks as though,
once again,
they're the "MAIN EVENT."

He's still not quite sure
if anyone wagered.

Fuck, he still questions their motives—intent.
And for good g'damn reason . . .

He's engaged in an infant cockfight!
Which of these leaves blessed those seeds
with their consent?

What the fuck!?
NOT AGAIN!
He's emotionally bent.

A drop of piss,
down his leg . . .
yep, he went.

He'd gotten so shook up,
that his Underoos . . .
he's slightly wet.

On the soggy Spiderman,
who'd place the first bet?

Understand . . .
this wasn't the first time
that they'd met—here.
Even though they're related,

this fruit fights as dirty
as a crabapple can get—fear.

Yes, he's scared.

'Cause, once again,
they've paired him with
the craziest of a fruit bully!

We swear on everythin'
this one's a nutcase,
that fell—flat on their core,
from the top of a full tree.

This is the only fight
of the night.
But it's the one
everyone loves
to cheer for, non-discreet.

They don't swing for too long
(they're not "one punch" strong)
before their bodies,
'n the floor,
they both greet.

He'd skinned both of his elbows,
his shoulder, 'n a knee,
when he left his feet.

The fruit starts to scratch,
'n bite, like he's a piece of meat.

He pulls the apple's stem,
(which infuriates them)
in a last-ditch attempt

to fully break free.

Just as a tiny window
of separation can be seen,
the apple lunges down towards his legs.
But grabs EVERYTHIN' in between.
Now he's swingin' away,
with all of his means.

You'd think that someone,
ANYONE,
would immediately intervene.

I mean, this perverted motherfucker's
still twistin' his frank around the beans!

"Aaah, somebody help!" he'd plead.
"PLEASE, GET HIS HANDS OFF OF MY PEEN!"

Finally . . .
(after his lengthy scream)
they jump—in between.

By way of disqualification,
he wins . . .
An unwanted victory, in the playpen,
versus the meanest of mean.

By this point, he just wants t'go
back to his branch, grab his teddy bear,
'n sleep away this strenuous memory,
that he'd love for his mind to wipe clean.

And for years, it had . . .

HUNG OVER

Although his body's always
been alcohol-free,
he's gotten drunk,
off of a case of tears.

He's huddled in a corner,
while they're cuddlin'
mixed drinks,
'n ice-cold beers.

Which, in most other trees,
it'd surely go over smoothly.
The outcome would be alright.

Everyone would laugh,
tell stories,
'n it'd turn out t'be
a fun-filled night.

But, this is the weekend
where he's already sick,
to a toilet's delight.

Stressed the fuck out.
Knowin' that this is the beginnin'
of what will most definitely end
in some sorta fight.

It's just a matter of when,
of who's initiated the process.
All seeds have been sent to bed.

He lays there with inquisitive ears,
tryin' to hear everythin'

they've done or said.

Keepin' one eye on the doorway
at all times.
Drunkenness scares him to death.

He's developed an anxiety
towards the slurrin' of conversations
accompanied by liquored breath.
He pretends t'be out cold,
often fallin' asleep distressed.

Doin' his best imitation of a corpse
once rigor mortis sets in,
post-death.

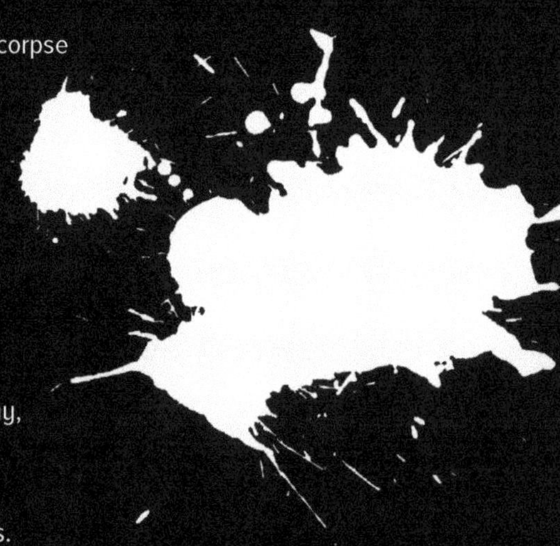

And, as expected . . .

they got up this A.M.,
to a post-party mess.

He avoided all of the anarchy,
'n woke up to this instead.

The floor's covered in towels.
And you'll never,
in a million years, guess
what their fish had been hand-fed . . .

take one guess.

Go ahead.

If you guessed
"a fuckin' boot,
right through the aquarium glass,"

then you were correct!

There was an alcohol-
related toilet burial.
All of their fish are dead.

No one's safe from the anarchy.
Not even a family pet.

He's huddled in a corner.
Gettin' drunk,
off of a case of tears.

Fuck this seedhood,
of grown-folk regrets!

BELLYACHIN' BEAT DOWNS

You just wait until
your leaf blows in . . .

God, he used to fear
those dreadful words.

If they did somethin',
ANYTHIN', wrong,
they'd be gettin' the belt.
You can rest assured!

But this leaf had a sinister method.

They'd let the seeds choose the weapon.

Which came with

an interestin' catch.

They could choose between:

"Big Brown"
and
"Thin Black."

You see, the size of the belt,
determined the number—of whacks.

Now, whenever they got into trouble,
one always had the other's back.

But . . .
this crazy li'l *bahstid*
had a spiteful,
yet comical,
knack to takin' those whacks.

An fear of the belt . . .
he seemed to lack.

'Cause he absolutely got a kick
out of talkin' back,
in the midst of his whacks.

He's all:

"Does that make you feel good?"

WHACK

"Do you feel a lot bigger now?"

WHACK

"Can I have another?"

WHACK

While the other seed's like:

"WHAT IN THE FACK!?"

(In his head—of course.
He's not tryin' to make this shit any worse.
So, don't jump the gun
'n call 9-1-1
or the hearse.
This episode isn't the first.
And it certainly won't be the last.)

Here's a sad, but truthful, fact:

His antics drew the attention
away from everyone else's whacks.

Although, he'd often felt
like a complete shit sack . . .

after tryin' so hard
to hold back
every "bellyaching" laugh.

He remembers bein' so thankful,
for those deliberate (comical) acts.

And also bein' able to sit,
with his ass cheeks—both in tact.

Well . . .
for the most part.

Got a giant wooden spoon, or fork,
around back?

WHACK

SHIT SHOW

They're makin' human fudgesicles.
I'm tellin' ya.
This apple's beyond fuckin' weird.

That *bahstid*'s got a twisted agenda.
The motive is abundantly clear.
Their fixation is rather queer.

Not sure how long
they'd been takin' turns.
But the end is approachin'—NEAR.

As a leaf abruptly opens the door.
Everyone stops.
In shock.
No words.
Blank stare

They can't believe their eyes.
One's ass-out,
drawers down,
slumped over a chair.

One by one these fuckin' apples appear
to have been experimentin'
on one another.

IN ‘n OUT—with a fuckin’ broomstick.
They’re each takin’ it . . .
IN THE REAR.

Yes, inside the derrière.

No, you read that shit correctly.

It still makes me sick to my stomach.
I just threw up, in my mouth—I swear.

That frickin’ branch of horrors
was a non-scripted nightmare.

But, for HIM . . .
this is just one of the MANY times,
that he’s thanked the Good Lord
that he wasn’t in that room right there.

From this God-awful experience
he had thankfully been spared.

Let this serve as a small indication
of what it’s like,
for a seed,
to grow up
in FEAR . . .

like he did.

CRAZY CAT LADY

This is the type of nightmare
that he relives in his dreams.

The ones where he wakes up
open-mouthed
but he can't get out the screams.

The cat 'o nine tails
gonna whip that ass.
One got cut,
'n thrown in the trash.

The cat 'o eight tails
gonna whip that ass.
One got cut,
'n thrown in the trash.

The cat 'o seven tails
gonna whip that ass.
Two got cut,
'n thrown in the trash.

The cat 'o five tails
gonna whip that ass.
Three got cut,
'n thrown in the trash.

The cat 'o two tails
gonna whip that ass.
Two got cut,
'n thrown in the trash.

No more tails
to whip that ass.
She's gonna improvise,
'n the scars are gonna last.

They fucked up,
'n now she's gotta take her pick.

She's gonna grab somethin.'
It's gonna happen quick.
That curtain rod, on the window sill,
should do the trick.

They stepped out of line,
'n her anger's been sparked.
He doesn't wanna peek.
This shit's 'bout to pop off.
That metal coat hanger's
gonna leave quite the mark.

Remember when I said
that this bitch was mean?
They just walked in.
What a fucked-up scene.
These poor seeds
are all kneelin'
on rice 'n beans.

Kneelin' . . .
on . . .
dry rice . . .
'n uncooked beans.

These punishments are
beyond obscene.
I think—by now,
you see what I mean?

But that's not the most
fucked-up encounter
that he's ever met.
There's one disturbin' situation
that he'll never fuckin' forget.

He hasn't seen this crazy since.
At least, not yet.

Than the one time that
the Boogie Ma'am ripped the fuckin' chord
out of an actively WORKIN' television set . . .

And whipped that ass.

He still wakes up
feelin' bad for all the seeds
that threw her tails
in the trash.

Well . . .
not one of 'em . . .
They deserve everythin'
that's comin' to their ass.

OPEN MOUTH, INSERT FOOT

Of all the fuckin' strangeness,
that runs through the tree,
this is one of the moments
that's always bothered a seed.

Whenever this leaf would visit,
they'd all be forced
to cover their feet.

But the leaves didn't want them
bein' too obvious about it.
They'd often prompt their seeds,
to try to keep it discreet.

Which just always seemed
like a rather odd request
for them t'be asked to meet.

I mean, they're just seeds.

As long as their
unmentionables are covered,
then that should be
more than appropriate attire,
for them to meet 'n greet.

The leaf-like paranoia
seems to have increased.

It was quite awkward,
for all, to say the least.

One leaf's extremely fidgety,
'n inconsistent when they speak.

Especially while their eyes
begin to wander.

"What the hell is wrong with this leaf!?"
he'd ponder . . .

As their attention seemed to have grown
increasingly fonder . . .

whenever "So 'n so" entered the room.

Towards the floor's vicinity
their eyes continually loom.

At this point they're fully consumed . . .

by some fuckin' (open-toed) sandals.

Of all the crazy-ass scandals
that they'd been exposed to.

Guess that seed chose to wear
the wrong type of friggin' shoe.

Especially around this "foot fetish" leaf,
as they've been affectionately called
by very few.

CUFFIN' SEASON

When he first heard of
"cuffin' season"
he was quite confused.

Because way back when . . .
I mean way, way back,
before reprimandin' a seed
was considered abuse . . .

"cuffing,"
as they knew it,
was this leaf's "signature," go-to move.

Very few others
fully understand their path.
Unless you took a stroll,
through seedhood,
in their shoes.

Whenever they'd walked slowly

in this leaf's way,
they'd get a "cuff,"
to quicken up their groove.

You see,
cuffin' had NOT A FUCKIN' THING
t'do with relationships,
'n everythin' t'do with their hand
greetin' the back of a seed's head
with excruciatin' news . . .

Cuffing:
[kuh•fing]
transitive verb
The child re-directive *smack*
that they most commonly used.

"I remember them cuffin' me so hard,
that even her slipper
would disapprove."

To this day,
he still walks
at a vigorous pace.
He never (fully) understood
their angst.

What the hell
were they tryin' to prove?

Where in the fuck
were they always in such a rush
to get their impatient ass to?

It's pretty sad,
when you're now a leaf,
waitin' for a seedhood cuff,
that no longer
comes through.

His mind is mentally screwed!

TRUTH BE TOLD

Not everythin', in life,
is exactly as it appears.
Each 'n every thought,
we calculatively configure.

This picture, for instance,
in the grand scheme of things,
is so, so very much BIGGER.

Just because we write
"**he,**" "**she,**" or even "**I**"
in regards to what
took place (at times)
on one of their branches,
doesn't necessarily implicate
a "parental figure."

They always had relatives,
'n friend's they called relatives,
in 'n out of the tree.

Most of whom
were quick to pull on

their emotional trigger.

So, when we say "So 'n so"
did "this 'n that" . . .
in several directions
you could (quite easily)
point the finger.

But, do your best
not to let it linger.

Some of those greedy *bahstid*s
have threatened to sue,
'n we'd hate to bestow upon you
their selfishness 'n vigor.

To this very day,
even their parents
don't know everythin'.
As they were threatened,
on a daily basis—not to tell.

And since it's been
so many years . . .
they never took time—like this—
just to sit, 'n dwell.

One of them "she"s
has since left this world.
But we're absolutely sure,
she's DOWN there—raisin' hell.

For most of their seedhood,
she was their most frequent sitter.

Yet, she took that role
far too personally,
actin' like the designated hitter.

It didn't matter if she missed you
once, twice, three times . . .
she wasn't at all a quitter.

I'll never forget the time
that they got fed up,
with all of her shit,
'n fuckin' bit her.

From that day forward,
towards them,
she became sadistically bitter.

And they'd feel that bitterness,
every time their freshly warmed ass
made contact—with the shitter.

Unlike that one time,
sittin' in the back seat,
thinkin' they were out of reach,
when a backhand—from the driver's seat
made all of their teeth fuckin' jitter.

They never even saw that shit.

Now,
if (for some reason) she couldn't make it,
to hit . . .

err . . .

we mean sit,

‘n they were in a pinch,
then they’d call in ANOTHER BITCH.

Guess you could call her
the “pinch hitter.”

Although her (at bat) percentage
wasn’t nearly as high.

All things considered.

Oh, then, there was the young sitter,
that figured she’d give it a try.
She’d invite over her boyfriends,
‘n they’d stay outside
the entire time—gettin’ high.

We say boyfriend*s*,
‘cause it wasn’t always the same guy.
They’d regularly come, ‘n they’d go.
Until one of them tragically died.

He remembers that day vividly.
Her entire shift, she cried.

They quickly figured out
the HOWs ‘n WHYs.

She didn’t return
after his demise.
What a blessin’—in disguise.

As, today, she’s headed
towards the same demise.

Which leads us to

their savin' grace.
Who didn't sit for them
nearly enough.

She'd never raise a hand
towards an ass, or a face.
She was well aware
that they'd already
had it rough—enough.

There wasn't any question
that the times had become
extremely tough.

They didn't always have a babysitter.
So, it was difficult (when they did)
to exhibit trust.

And he wasn't in any
particular rush
to catch another
(back of the head)
"open cuff."

STATUTE OF LIMITATIONS

Growin' up,
all of his favorite nursery rhymes
were straight to the point
'n hard hittin'.

Which is why he felt
(for this particular thought)
that this style would be more

than appropriately fittin'.

ahem

Hey, fiddle fiddler!
How do you spot a diddler?

When they're the least likely
of suspected individuals
that you'd think to find.

Never thought this could
be a possibility—intertwined.

Yet, here we are.
Coincidentally . . .
there's more than one of a kind.

Nah, fuck it . . . y'know what?
I've changed my g'damn mind.
We can't be this fuckin' kind.
I'm done keepin' this thought
so uncomfortably confined.

It's time to flip the script,
on this particular poetic grind.

FUCK THESE PREDATORS
'n the facades
that they've been
hidin' behind.

Both underage, at the time.
Their leaves were
equally, ignorantly, blind.

As he screamed,

"FUCK YOU!
AND
FUCK YOU!
DON'T LIKE IT?
YOU CAN BOTH
COME MEET ME . . .

YES, BOTH OF YOU
FUCKIN' PERVERTS
ARE MORE THAN WELCOME,
TO COME 'N GREET ME.

Kickin' your asses,
usin' only my hands,
is the only way
you'll ever de-feet me.

'Cause the two of you
pussies combined,
have not a shot in hell
to exchange fists,
in order to defeat me."

Shots fired . . .
startin' on the left side
of this damn-near
obsolete tree.

Supposedly, a creeper was this weed.
An unwillin' participant was that seed,
as they'd (later in life) concede.

We believe the weed could be headed to Hell,
for what they tried to tell

about how said weed ruined their infancy,
completely.

But it was a leaf that said,
"Go back to bed!
They're just playin' around!"
Not so discreetly

Another contribution
towards the shamin'
of this tainted tree.

You can imagine the disbelief
when their livin' nightmare
made it's way back full of grief.

All along they'd known them t'be vile.
Unquestionably, livin' in denial.
What a secret to keep, internally.

They should've had
that weed's ass locked up,
'n thrown away the infernal key.

This late night,
moonlight,
wolf in pups' clothin',
against their will imposin',
purity of a seed-stealin'
nocturnal THIEF!

A fuckin' cock sucker,
that should be hung
from that fubar of a tree,
for the entire world to see.

But this wouldn't be
the only instance of diddln',
that would affect him—personally.

'Cause there's one other,
who'd "forcefully smother" another,
on a different branch that hangs
from this godforsaken tree . . .
This weed's as fucked up,
as bein' fucked up—can be.
The level of crazy is certifiably.
They should have locked that weed's
li'l seed-lovin' ass up,
'n also thrown away THAT key.

Inducin' fear was their specialty.
They preyed on those small as can be
in search of some forcibly obtained booty.
Threatenin' them with harm—bodily.
No stranger to sodomy.
This weed likes to bottom feed.

There was always somethin'
extremely dysfunctionally wrong,
with this sadistic scum of a weed!

From a leaf's immediate supervision
they should've never been freed . . .
into another's home—then left alone.
I still can't believe that weed went on to breed!?

What in the hell is wrong
with this bloodline,
that they internally bleed?!?

The tree's forever disgusted,

by both of your misdeeds.

If they could go back,
they'd pluck both of you weeds,
feed you to the goats,
'n fuckin' reseed.

FRICK 'N FRACK

Frick 'n Frack
packed a sack,
'n ventured out—on a journey.

Frick received (extensive) time.
Frack has reached "the end of his line."
While their victim wound up on a gurney.

What the fuck, man!?
Frick's gonna need an attorney.

The exact details,
in regards to this memory,
he finds too concernin'.

So, the vast majority . . .
we're goin' to avoid.

As you can imagine,
incarceration isn't a stranger.
It was introduced, to the tree,
when he was a young boy.

Other members play too closely to danger.
From petty larceny, 'n assault . . .

to kidnappin', 'n fraud.
Those flashin' lights—to some
are a symbol of "killjoy."

On this particular day,
the phone rings—in the kitchen.
The household's comfort level,
immediately, begins to deploy.

There's plenty of confusion,
as questions are asked.
Someone makes mention of
what he'd describe now as a police convoy.

Frick's committed a serious offense.
In fact, when this story completely ends,
more than one life will have been destroyed.

Sounds like their victim's a younger kid.
Whom they thought they'd left—well hid.
Now everyone's prayin' that
he's gonna pull through—'n live.

'Cause Frick, 'n Frack,
are each facin' a lengthy bid.

This is no time to play dumb, nor act coy.

As they're lookin' through windows, without views,
'n walkin' through doors, without freedom.
They've been read their rights.
But . . .
they've also been known to mistreat 'em.

They should have been honest, from the start.
Yet they felt an urgency to flee, 'n mislead 'em.

As Frack couldn't deal
with the charges he'd face.

What happens next,
some might consider a disgrace.

He's terminated his own life . . .
Strangulation—by way of a shoe lace.

Now Frick is in
(even more) serious trouble.

With Frack deceased
his bid's about to double.

He's committed a crime.
So, he's gotta do hard time . . .

While Frack will be buried—
beneath dirt, 'n rubble.

OH NO THEY DIDN'T

These crab apples are at it again.
When it comes to apples,
there's a simple explanation.

This is but one, of the many that he's formed.

While some seeds become leaves
he tends to believe—that from the tree,
some apples were born.

You know what they say about apples:

"One bad one spoils a bunch."
"They don't fall far from the tree."
"As sour as they come."
"Rotten to the core."

In this case,
those sayings apply—'n more.
Individually
arguably
non–gender-specifically.

You get the picture, I'm sure.

Screamin' 'n arguin' . . .
They're 'bout to bring the drama.

It's an all-out onslaught of an
awkwardly unbearable game of
"Yo Mama."
Now he's not old enough—to play along.
But, even if he were, he quickly realizes
they've chosen their opponents
ALL WRONG!

The little one starts off with a major burn.
"YO MAMA'S LIKE A DOOR KNOB . . .
WE'VE ALL HAD A TURN!"
gasp

Tall 'n lanky's up next,
Tryin' to one-up that slow squab.
They yell out:
"YO MAMA'S LIKE A HAIR DRYER . . .
SHE JUST GAVE ME A BLOW JOB!"
cringe

For what lasted far too long,
they'd continue t'go back 'n forth.
A low blow down south.
An uppercut to the north.

The blasphemy finally comes
to an abrupt end,
with an even grosser retort:
"LET'S GET OFF OF MOTHERS . . .
BECAUSE I JUST GOT OFF OF YOURS!"
ewwww

When it comes to levels of ignorance,
there's no low to which they won't resort.

If this were any type of an intelligence mission,
they'd all have been screamin'—**ABORT! ABORT!**

But he felt like a field mouse
who's been filled by
a fully grown elephant's girth.
I mean, as far as feelin' awkwardly uncomfortable,
he couldn't possibly think of anythin' worse.

Except possibly watchin' these
SEEDS
go back 'n forth,
about what they'd hypothetically done
with **THEIR OWN LEAF**,
by way of sexual intercourse.

Epic YO MAMA fail!
Brought to you by this tree . . .
of course.

BREAKFAST PROBLEMS

Woke up this A.M.
to chaos 'n strife.

One's got the other straddled,
wieldin' a knife.

"Drunken Anarchy"—

that could be another title
to his fucked-up life.

Who does a seed speak to
regardin' an intervention?

They've got some strong intentions.

He needs somebody—anybody
to intervene.

We're talkin' somebody
to step in between.

'Cause he's not fuckin' doin' it!

Can someone responsible
sort this all out, for him, please?

He needs somebody who can answer
this inquisition responsibly.

"Is there anyone out there
that cares to respond,
to a seed—in need?"

A response to this question
is really all that he's lookin' for,
indeed.

He's not lookin' for a
lengthy correspondence.

Hell,
he'd even settle for more
of a core respondent . . .

To determine whose
responsibility it was
to delegate their
responsibilities.

How the fuck
can he be raisin' them,
when they're supposed t'be
seed raisin' leaves!?

We'll wait . . .

Raisin' his "adults" . . .
what the fuck is up with that!?

It's an awkward situation,
to experience these roles
crossin' paths.

They're supposed t'be
the "grownups" . . .
but they've both been
showin' their ass.

In a metaphorical sense . . .

like showin' off for the class.

Who the hell does he turn to?

They're supposed t'be
the ones that he'd ask.

AND . . .

to top it all off,
everyone, on the outside,
has an opinion . . .

yet, none of them care
to hear—any of the facts.

When all he would've liked
was some sort of "normal,"
accompanied by peaceful acts.

Oh . . .
and some cereal.

If that's not too much—to ask.

SEPARATED

You were supposed to
be his best friend.
How the fuck could
you just leave?

He woke up 'n you were gone.

No goodbye.
Nor even a letter.
No explanation (of your absence)
did he receive.

He spent the whole day
in that frickin' window.
Not one time did he see,
your car pass by the apartment,
on his street.

Where the fuck can you be?

While your ass is out,
amongst the stars,
he fuckin' cries himself
to sleep!

He knows you'll be home
any time now.

Right!?

I mean,
this all has t'be
a really bad dream.

He feels like it's all his fault.
He's placed the blame
on himself, it seems.

What could he have changed?
What could he have possibly
done differently?

He picked up all of his toys.

His bedroom is
all the way clean.

You can come home
any time now.

It's been an eternity.

He can feel it in his heart.
How could he be so naive?

He thought you were inseparable.
Boy, was he deceived.

She told him that he's now
the "man of the house."

He's still unsure
what the fuck
that shit means . . .

Where are you!?

PLANTIN' SEEDS

He's a "born-again bastard"!

A feat that he's kinda,
sorta,
mastered.

He's been disowned
a time,
or three.

Or four?

T'be honest,
he doesn't really keep count
anymore.

Nonetheless . . .

rumors,
to this seed's psyche,
have been an utter disaster.
Some of which
have shaken him,
to the depths
of his core.

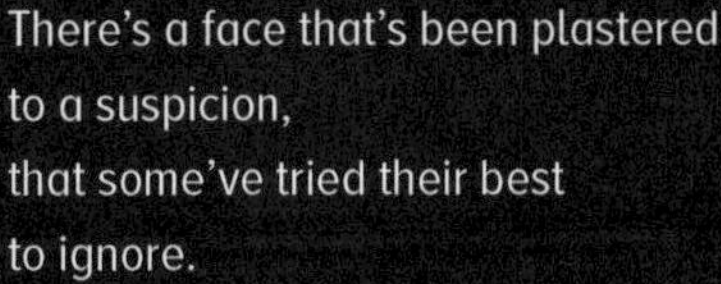

There's a face that's been plastered
to a suspicion,
that some've tried their best
to ignore.

It appears to have been
a difficult task, for all involved,
to succeed.

Since, **THAT** seed might be related.

There's a slight possibility
that they've "branched off"
of our tree—indeed.

It goes without sayin' that a DNA test
they, adamantly, felt was in need.

Because some are in denial,
when it comes to that wild

. . .ly grown sunflower seed.

They might,
very well,
BE one of **WE**.

Which could've been a reach, to heed.

Although,
if you looked really closely,
they appeared to have his eyes,
his hair,
'n his nose.

But what the hell would this seed know,
about how that seed grows . . .
up—if he hasn't, yet, been told?!

I mean . . .
he's on a visitation,
in a leaf's cohabitated household.

Which was an easy transition,
towards what would unfold.

Because she used to babysit for . . .
long pause

Which would mean that . . .
longer pause

Ohhhhhhhhhhhhhhhhhhhhhhhhhh!

MAKE A WISH

Divorce taught them many lessons.
Especially when it came time
to find somethin' to eat.

And when I mention the word find,
I mean that shit **LITERALLY** . . .

When you've got
to fend for yourselves,
'n selection of food
is lookin' bleak,
you turn into a "Scraps MacGyver"
with any of the condiments
that leak.

They quickly discovered
"wish sandwiches."

I'm sure you've heard of them.
There's no need for me
t'be discreet.

They always had some
sort of stale(ish) bread.
But they wished that
they had some meat!

Those that know the struggle,
can relate to this situation
wholeheartedly.

He's gotta feed the other seeds.

As the man of the house . . .
that's part of his responsibilities.

Although,
he's not allowed to use a knife.
So, they use things that they can
scoop out,
or squeeze.

Sometimes if they got lucky,
inside of the fridge,
they'd find a brick of orange cheese!

But not today.
Mayonnaise sandwich for them.
Ketchup for them.
And a syrup sandwich for him, please.

And they ALWAYS used the crusts.
Those were hot commodities.

They learned not to waste a crumb.
On every last morsel
they would feed.

Right now they don't have much.
But they have everythin' they need . . .

for lunch.

FAST FOOD DUDE

They often brought their seeds
to each other's houses.

At times, for several hours,
they'd stay.

While the leaves hung out,
'n shot the shit,
their seeds would run around—'n play.

You should know that . . .
sometimes the other seeds
cracked him the fuck up,
with the shit they'd often do—'n say.

He may have been young at the time,
but he still laughs at this experience
like it was yesterday.

That dude's got his first job,
'n today—he's cashin' out
his first week of pay.

He's lookin' all disheveled—
in his wrinkled khaki pants,
matchin' collared shirt,
topped off with a visor . . .
'n his hair's all in disarray.

Complete with the fresh aromas
of flame-broiled burgers,
over a slight hint
of fish filet.

Yet, he's still feelin' fine,
all dressed up to work the line.
The dude was reppin',
to the fullest,
that burger joint—all day.

A leaf says to the dude,
"Hey, you're lookin' pretty sharp!
What time do you work?
Are you headed on your way?"

To which the dude would proudly say,
"What's today, Saturday?
Nah . . . it's my day off.
I don't have to
go into work—today!"

Wait, **WHAT**!?

. . . the hell did he just say?

long pause

Anyone else thinkin'
Employee of the Frickin' Month?

Fuckin' A!

THIS dude . . .
sportin' the uniform,
on his day off!?

OY VEY . . .

DO OVER

How did I become so
g'damn depressed?

Why can't "I" just say

some shit—in jest?

Why should my thoughts
remain suppressed?

When can I sleep?
I need some rest.

Constantly writin'
under duress.

I feel like a damsel
in distress.

'Cause I've "BROAD-ened" my mind,
with this S.O.S.

Someone save me,
from my inopportune—openness.
Please . . .
fuck this pain,
felt in my chest.

Fuck all those half-truths,
THEY'VE said "in jest."

Fuck a book,
written while depressed.

Fuck the **C**ompulsive **D**isorder,
over which I've overly **O**bsessed.

Fuck these feelings,
my God—I'm stressed.

Fuck every topic,

that I've already fuckin' addressed.
Fuck all of those memories,
that STILL (and always will)
remain oppressed.

Someone take me away,
from this cluster-fucked
mental mess.

This mentalness.
Please . . .

Fuck . . .
This life, it can't be meant
for a guy who'd give up everythin',
to live a single day
without regrets.

Somewhere, I've gone wrong.
It shouldn't have taken this long.

Today I feel like breakin' down,
some shit that they've beset.

Sort of a redo—of some of the shit
that they'll someday regret.

Life, with this tree,
could have been so
much more tolerable . . .
if it came with a button
I could "press to reset" . . .

I'd press that fuckin' button
every chance that I'd get!

I guess it'd be safe to bet,
that I have many reasons why
I'm so mentally g'damn upset . . .

Fuck all of this shit!

[RESET]

FEEL THE DARKNESS

Drown in my eyelids.
Suffocate in my mind.
Hang from my subconscious thoughts.
Get burnt by the memories—you hesitantly find.

Suicidal tendencies.
Homicidal bind.

Metaphorical death sentencin'.
Chloroforically designed.

Pass out—on my sadness.
Curl up—into a ball.

Crashed out—from the madness.
Missed the writin'—on the wall.

Carved from the same tree.
Not far—does the apple ever fall.

Roll all around—in all of their bullshit.
Smell the aroma—of my withdrawal.

Awaken, in a frantic mind state—no escape . . .

all you can muster up, is a limp attempt—to crawl.

And in THAT moment's end,

Then, and ONLY then—will you fully comprehend . . .
How desperate he feels—
whenever he cowers, at night, to bawl.

You can take the boy out of the city,
but the city's already done scarred him,
FOR LIFE . . .

The memories cut deep—like a knife.
Submerged below the surface.
Diggin' in—with a purpose.
Unburyin' the past—is the therapeutic vice.

At night, he's all done pissin' the bed.
Now, he's pissin' in bottles—instead.
The darkness has fucked—with his head.
Those things that go "bump" in the night—aren't ever nice.

Out there lies

. . . many drunken nights,
. . . many brutal fights,
. . . many tearful sights,
. . . many unbearable frights.

"Please, DON'T TURN OFF THE LIGHTS!"

"I'm beggin' you . . . PLEASE! Not tonight."

click

He's not leavin' his room.

He's sleepin' with his ass (pressed firmly)
against the back wall.

He's not a fan—of the doom 'n gloom.
He's keepin' an ear (fully attentive)
towards the back hall.

"I hope I brought enough bottles—to consume.
I'm not goin' anywhere near that bathroom stall."

Stall—for as long as it takes.
Stall—until the sunrises, 'n daylight breaks.

He's not goin' anywhere, in the darkness—AT ALL.

OLIVE BRANCH OF HOPE

It's crazy how much
times have changed
from the eighties,
to the teens.

What the hell happened,
to the neighborhood,
in that period of time
in between?

Nowadays, you wouldn't even think
about feedin' your seeds
to those streets.

They'd be chewed up,
spit out,
'n then checked

for heartbeats.

But as for them . . .
they were thrown from the nest.
None of them were ever weaned.

It was an unspoken understandin'.
You could call it a "steady routine."

From the time the sun rose
in the mornin' . . .
'til dusk,
when the street lights
would come to a gleam.

They'd be outside playin',
with their friends.

From the "House of Friendliness,"
to the other side of the city,
'n everywhere else
in between.

Occasionally they'd make
their way back home,
if they found the time
for lunch.

But their pickings there were scarce.
So, that didn't happen
very much.

Luckily for himself,
'n the other seeds,
they had leaves scattered
around the block.

Their grandleaf,
for instance,
was a mere five-minute walk.

And around the corner
from her house . . .
well, that's where they'd like
this thought
to officially start.

That's where she lived.
The girl of every nine-
'n ten-year-old's dreams.

She was pretty,
liked sports,
'n (most importantly)
when no one else did,
she paid attention to **this** seed.

Now we're not settin' this up
as a love story,
or anythin' that
would end romantically.

We're talkin' about a great friend,
who was there,
without ever even knowin' it,
in the beginnin'
of his time of need.

And, for that,
he's eternally grateful
for his (longtime)
seedhood friend, D.T.

TAPPED YET UNROOTED

Everyone should have
at least one friend
who encourages
this kind of hope.

Who brings somethin'
into their life
that makes it easier
to cope . . .
with all of the issues,
they struggle with
day after day.

To be a shoulder to lean on,
'n show them that
(no matter what they're dealin' with)
"everything's gonna be okay."

They didn't really talk
about his home,
or the divorce,
or anythin' of the sorts.
She took his mind
away from the heartache,
by enticin' his love of sports.

With two baseball gloves,
'n a ball,
his woes disappeared
for hours at a time.

Her friendship gave him somethin'
positive to look forward to.
An olive branch of hope,
to leave the negativity behind.

And for as long as
it was open . . .
in that difficult period
of time,
through that window
he would climb.

Lifelong friends,
like her,
are a rarity to find.

Which is why,
when he needed one the most,
he believes that God made her
one of a kind.

He's FOREVER grateful—for this time
. . . even well after they moved away.

GOLDEN GLOVES OFF

Bein' "the man of the house"
just doesn't feel right.

He was ill prepared,
for this type of strife.

Everything's so different,
since that leaf's gone.
They're experiencin' a
different way of life.

He's frantically awoken,
from a deep sleep,

with sudden fright.

And now it's his job
to check on the things,
that go bump—in the night.

What if they have a gun!?
What if they're carryin' a knife!?
But what he's about to encounter,
he can't stand the sight.

There's loud screamin',
'n commotion.
Tensions are at an
extremely volatile height.

These two leaves
are 'bout t'go all in.

IT'S A FRANTIC FISTFIGHT!

"So 'n so's with me!"
"I'm with So 'n so!"
"Get your own!"
"Why do you always steal mine!?"
'n more . . .

It would appear that
they've been in this
situation before.

They're inside the house,
standin' in front of
the back door.

In an inner hallway,

that's ridiculously thin.

Against the wall they're
both conspicuously pinned.

This is when he sees fists
begin to take flight.

There's hands full of hair.
Pushin' 'n pullin' everywhere.
He can't separate them.
He gives it all of his might.

They're cryin', *"Stop."*
He's cryin', *"Let go."*
She just let out
her first curse word.
This shit isn't fuckin' right!

They can't get these leaves apart.
Their hands are clingin'
to each other's scalps,
'n clenched,
far too hella tight.

On one leaf's foot, there's a cast.
It's kickin' some serious ass.
More literally, cast to face.

Before they can swing' 'em,
their crutches, he quickly takes.

They're a couple of small seeds.

Smack dab in the middle,
of grown-folk mistakes.

The landlord barged in,
with a bat.

Finally . . .
the altercation breaks.

He can hear the sirens.
The cops are on their way.

"Man of the house" in full effect.
Holdin' a couple o' leaves
at bay.

HOLY HELL!

GOVERNMENT-FUNDED SNACKS

Some of my weirdest
seedhood memories
wouldn't have involved
any sort of bribery . . .

one would think.

But, you know what!?

It's really quite astonishin'
how quickly one's morals
can stoop,
or shrink.

Sometimes a leaf
(to get them out of their hair,
t'go anywhere—but there),

would toss them a buck
or two . . .
'n a suspect wink.

Which he'd quickly
toss into his pants pocket,
(without ever lookin' at it)
with a fast crumple,
'n a crink.

You never wanna give 'em
time—to reconsider.

They could change their minds,
'n your "hush money"
would be gone,
within a blink.

Runnin' out the door,
head down,
feet racin' towards the store.

"Do we want,
Café Espresso (for some fries)
or
John & Son's (for a sausage link)?"

"Nah . . .
I'm not gettin' either.
I want somethin' else—I think."

He digs into his pocket . . .
look down

holy shit!
pause

The dollar . . .
pause

it's fuckin' PINK!
quickly closin' his hand

We're not talkin' Monopoly PINK.
You know . . .
don't pass GO.
Head directly to the clink,
without collectin' the currency
that gets transported
by a fictional Brinks truck—PINK.

We're talkin' motherfuckin' food-stamp PINK!

He can immediately
feel his face turnin' red,
'n his heart begin to sink.
looks around

"What the fuck
are all of his friends
gonna say?"

Better yet,
what the hell
will everyone else think?

And what if they tell people
at the House of Friendliness about this,
like some blabbermouth of a fink?

Man, that shit
would really frickin' stink!

Damn . . .

All he really wanted
was some cheese doodles,
'n a nice cold drink.

Fuck it . . .
"Real Men Pay with Pink."

Yeah, that's what he's tellin' himself.
Just play along—
wink, wink

"ORANGE" BADGE OF COURAGE

When I heard them rhyme words like:
orange, porridge, four-inch,
door hinge, and storage . . .
I thought, *"Our tree can a buck-ten relate!"*

What if I add my own flare, to create?
If I may step a bowl up to the plate.

When he refers to "porridge" . . .
what he's really referrin' to is:
stale oatmeal,
drownin' in lukewarm
Worcester water,
if that was all
that he could forage,
when there was a shortage
of the cereal they'd normally ate.

It's an act,

that he'd highly discourage—at any rate.

But if he **MUST** . . .

he'd introduce a
two- (or
more) inch
orange
to his porridge.

Since it was the only fruit
left in iceboxed storage . . .

But the poor fridge
is usually
runnin' on empty . . .

since that one time
when he accidentally
spilt the last of
his porridge
on the floor 'n
it left an
orange-floor tinge.

"You'd better clean it all up,
or you're gonna be sorry!
Don't tempt me."

He'd sick to his core cringe,
if that orange
led to a sore binge
of his ass,
at the tail end
of a belt,
or a slipper.

They weren't orange,
nor fringe . . .
yet they sure
kick-started his endorphins
while wonderin'
which it was gonna be:
the black, leather,
or
the yellow, slip-on,
ass-whipper!?

He supposed that
either one was better
than bein' hit with
an orange store wrench,
or a scuba divin' flipper.

Right!?

For the better part
of a year,
he lived in fear,
of that g'damn slipper.

Even more so if
it came anywhere near
several empty cans of beer.
No, they weren't a sipper.

That's when he learned
the importance of
an orange door hinge,
as they almost busted it off
like J. the g'damn Ripper
wieldin' a fuckin' slipper.

Okay, it was a rusty
copper color,
but you get the frickin' picture.

At least the door is still
an upright
(yet, now, opened) fixture.

And his ass
is about to become
a magnificent
red, yellow, black 'n blue MIXTURE!

Looks like he's takin'
another one for the team—blister.

SHARIN' IS CARIN'

Home's gotten rough,
rather quickly.

The cabinetries are lookin' bleak.

Since divorce moved into the tree,
they're livin' off of a different
scenario—each week.

At times, the cupboards are scarce.
His stomach is bare,
'n the fridge starts lookin' meek.

They all got up
this mornin'
lookin' for breakfast.

I mean . . .
they're young seeds.
They want to eat.

But (on this day) there's
maybe a cup of milk,
and just barely enough
cereal—for three.

So,
they'd start with just
what they felt they'd need:
one bowl,
one spoon,
'n hopefully there's enough
generic shredded wheat.

Youngest
to oldest
is the peckin' order.

They just hope that
it'll fit their need.

Let's call them "First Milk,"
since they'd eat first,
there's no room
for any greed.

Their sole job is to leave
enough milk behind,
in the bowl, for the others
to also feed.

"Second Milk" is up next.
They've gotta try to pull off

that same exact milk feat.

By pourin' their cereal
into the leftover milk . . .
while leavin' enough milk behind,
in the bowl
(when they're done eatin'),
for "Third Milk" to also eat.

He always ate last.

They looked to him
to make that call.

He's the "man of the house."

As such,
it's now his job,
to sacrifice for them all.

Even if it means goin' hungry . . .
"Third Milk" sufferin' breakfast withdrawal.

51773

The numbers 51773 belong
to a numerical sequence,
that he discovered—as a child

on one of the many occurrences
when he was bein' punished,
for actin' "out of control, 'n wild."

This comin' from a drunken leaf . . .

who's been meanderin' through life—in denial.

But at least, today, he hasn't caught the slipper,
'cause that shit's ALWAYS gruesome—so vile.

He once thought he was gonna
be beaten to death—no trial.
"Dead seed walkin'" **fo' sho'!**
Green Mile

The one time he thought he'd
twist 'n miss the blow—agile.
Instead he flinched 'n got hit low—penile.

Which had a nine-year-old's (freshly)
whooped ass talkin' off 'n slow—senile.

But not today! Ain't happenin'! Noooooo! Argyle.
Sent abruptly to his bedroom cell . . .
non-stop, all GOOOOOO! Exile.

No TV.
No toys.
No fun.
No choice.

"You must really hate me!" he said.
"Now I've got nothin' to play with!" he pled.
thinkin' his age *"I may as well just be dead . . ."*

Solitary confinement, he dreads
while sittin' on the edge of his bed.
Thoughts racin' all through his head.
After push ups 'n sit ups, he's shred.
All of his books, he's read.
What the heck can he do instead?

think
look
think

GOT IT!

On the floor, he finds a calculator to use.
Hey, it's somethin' to clear a seed's blues!

So, he starts fiddlin' 'round—spellin' words
by usin' the numbers as lettered clues.
Like: *Ohhh, LOOSE, hOES*, 'n *BOOBS*.

*don't judge . . .

Of course, he knew about boobs—prepubes.
. . . Don't even get us started on their "sock drawer nudes,"

which weren't taken the same time that those
leaves were in their kitchen smokin' doobs.

*tokin' buds . . .

Those came after family feuds.
Shit . . .

For most of y'all,
this shouldn't come as any new news.

YES . . . he witnessed some isht—for you newbs,
while fetchin' rum 'n Cokes 'n ice-cold brews.

Which brings us full circle, back around
to that calculator, that he found, on the ground.
Post-drunken sentencin', boredom-bound.

What he discovered, he thought t'be quite profound.
The number's 51773 defined his exile island,
when he looked at them upside-down!

He's a rhythmical, numerical, grammatical, genius . . .
(DAMN! We kinda like the way that sounds.)
Or just extremely bored . . .
on a calculator . . .
playin' 'round—either way.

Inmate 51773—House Renowned

REGRETFULLY YOURS

It's kinda funny,
how everyone always says
they want what's best for you . . .

that is, until what's best for you,
becomes non-beneficial—to THEM.

a—hh—hh—hem

I'm-a regret not spittin' out
that phlegm.

"I hope he doesn't write
anythin' that he'll regret."

Gosh, I knew there was
somethin' that I'd forget.

No, really . . .

I'm expected to make
some people fret.

I mean, they haven't even read
a single sentence, yet,
'n I've already gotten
them upset?!

They know that I'm ear-to-ear
in subconscious debt . . .
'n still expect me to default
on these back thoughts I get.

Nah . . .
never that . . .
I'm all set.

You wouldn't believe
half the shit that
the mind chooses
to forget.

But the truth is:
The more I start to remember,
the more regretful I can get
(for everyone involved).

Like . . .
I regret not stoppin'
all of their verbal,
physical,
'n mental,
abuse.

I regret watchin' a leaf
turn itself into

a bedridden recluse.

I regret every time
they chose to beat
his body—head to ass.

I regret him havin' to duck
out of the way
of that flyin' glass.
The entire porcelain collection,
bein' thrown at his adolescent ass,
by a drunken lass.

I regret them tellin' people
that he was "mouthy,
'n out of control."

I regret that they couldn't see,
that their substance abuse
(on his young psyche)
was just takin' a substantial toll.

I regret all of the nights
that he went to sleep,
with his heart filled with hate . . .
'cause they were out
spendin' money on others
while they barely had food
on their plate.

"Such 'n such" again . . .
no meat.
Well, that's just fuckin' great!
(But, at least on those nights,
they all ate. Amen.)

Scared, sleepless nights . . .
alcohol, in a flask.

For every time that slipper
left a foot,
I regret him not bein'
a little,
just a tad bit,
more fast.

And, in his slowness,
I regret him hidin' under the bed . . .
what a dumbass
'n bein' dragged out
by both his fuckin' legs.

Another senseless beatin',
that started in the bedroom
'n ended in that narrow hallway,
with his entire body bein' pegged.

I regret that leaf havin' to leave
them all behind,
even though (for them)
they all had begged.

Three strikes 'n that leaf was tossed out . . .
like their breakfast—burnt egg.

Eventually they'd return to home plate.

But that was
AFTER
the shit
had already
hit the keg.

ROACH OR FAMINE

Their stomachs are loudly grumblin',
while the cockroaches
appear t'be gettin' fatter.

When you turn on
a dark room's light,
they should all begin
to scatter.

As if you dropped
a porcelain plate
on the floor,
'n watched
all of the little pieces
shatter.

They're everywhere you look.
It doesn't really matter.

But . . .

if you enter a room,
'n the roaches look back at you
like you're disturbin' **THEIR** peace . . .

then you're growin' up straight "hood."
Like they did, as seeds. Sublease.

Even the fuckin' roaches had attitudes.
Not a care in the g'damn world.

He could share numerous occasions
where he's gagged, teared up, 'n hurled.

Like that day
when he was eatin'
right out of the box,
of generic Raisin Bran.

No need for a spoon,
he was diggin' in
with his hand.
They didn't have any more milk.
So, you've gotta take
what you can take.

He reached back into the box,
'n the raisins began to run
beneath the flakes.

He quickly came to realize,
that it wasn't a raisin
that he'd just ate.

He probably should've known,
by the unexpected crunch.

Or by that nasty taste.

Another good one,
gone too soon.

One that can't soon be replaced.

Wrong box.
Wrong time.
I guess you could call it
"an untimely waste"
of a box of cereal.

I'm pretty sure he'd hate
for me to cut this thought short.
But I'm also sure that he doesn't
wanna lose his place.

His bug is up next.
It's goin' down

ROACH RACE!

NEVER HAVE I EVER

So many things goin' on
inside of my head
that I don't like to rethink.

I couldn't possibly elaborate
on every fucked-up situation
without us both needin' a shrink.

So . . .
since that tree loves to play games
(that really aren't so clever), how
about a quick little game called
"Never Have I Ever"?

He'll start . . .

Never have I ever
thrown a seed out of the house
"the same way that they
came into this world":
totally NUDE.

Never have I ever
forced a seed to consume
everythin' on their plate,
by pushin' their entire face
INTO THEIR FOOD.

Never have I ever
poured scaldin' hot water,
into a leaf's lap—out of sheer rage.

Never have I ever
said that a relative
chewin' bubble gum
off of the sidewalk
was just goin' through a stage.

Never have I ever
withheld the passin' of a leaf,
from the rest of the tree,
post-death.

Never have I ever
pretended t'be Santa Claus,
on Christmas Eve,
carryin' a bag filled with
McDonald's dollar-menu toys,
with cheap liquor on my breath.

Never have I ever
left any seeds outside alone,
while a spouse wasn't home,
so that I could "entertain" a neighbor.

Never have I ever
gotten anyone in trouble,
by committin' fraud,

in terms of labor.

Never have I ever
been so alarmed by a knock at the door,
that I (while armed with a shotgun)
made the now-panic-stricken seeds
hide behind the giant picture tube
box TV that sat directly on the floor.

Never have I ever
disrespected any seeds
by tellin' them,
"Your leaf is nothin' more than a whore."

Never have I ever
locked any seeds in a dark basement,
yellin'—"*The rats are comin!"*—
while makin' scratchin' noises
outside of the door.

Never have I ever
competed with a spouse,
to see who could kiss a
female "better"
(based upon a hunch?).

Never have I ever
knocked a preteen seed out cold,
"just tryin' to see if they
could take a punch."

Never have I ever
made a seed wear their underwear,
inside-out, on top of their head,
as a form of punishment.

Never have I ever
taken all of the leftovers out of the fridge,
mixed them together (in a giant fryin' pan),
called that vile concoction "hash,"
then served it to the tree—for nourishment.

Never have I ever
threatened to sue a family member,
for writin' a book of thoughts
based upon their tree/upbringin',
by tryin' to use fear as discouragement.

Never have I ever
placed any form of poisonin'
into the tree's meal.

Never have I ever
stumbled through three backyards,
tryin' to dip from a cabby
who came knockin' on the back door
lookin' for his cab fair . . .
while laughin' hysterically
after witnessin' (then explainin')
the entire drunken ordeal.

This shit is so fuckin' real . . . SMH.
I can honestly say that never have **I** ever
done any of the above.
"Hooray, I'm so elated!"

But if **YOU** couldn't raise your hand
(for all of the above)
then WE could possibly be related . . .

Nah . . .

HUNGRY MAN . . . ERR, BOY

Thinkin' back to the days
when he was a helluva lot thinner.

T'those nights when
they had nothin' to consume,
but sleep for dinner.

Fuck . . .
that sucked.

Out of all of the
alphabetical possibilities,
for a preteen, cabinet-robbin'
sinner . . .

*zZzZzZz*s were quite often
a landslide winner.

I wonder if they grew up
in a similar way?

If their leaves knowingly
kept their appetites
at bay.

That would explain
why one stabbed their seed,
in the forehead,
over a piece of meat
that fucked-up day.

Imagine watchin'
this heinous display?

"This year's Hunger Games—
sponsored by Chik-f'n-A!"

Nada
Zip
Zilch

Not even a scrap 'n
I'm tryna make light
of these memories
into which I'm tappin'.

Unfortunately, this really
did happen.

All of the above—I should say.

A grumblin' stomach
is the narrator,
from this bed—that I lay.

Several times,
he'd manage to drift
'n fade away.

Only t'be awoken,
by the sounds
of his stomach's
one-person play.

"An appetite worth discussin'."

A tale of complete,
'n utter dismay.

Someone pass him

one of those sheep,
that baa-baa-baa-bounce
as he counts each servin'
of lambchops, pre-sleep,
that he'd like to slay!

He's been tryin' to fill himself up . . .
in his dreams . . .
if he may.

'Cause dreamin' of eatin'
is the only way he's grubbin'
today.

SHIT BRICK ROAD

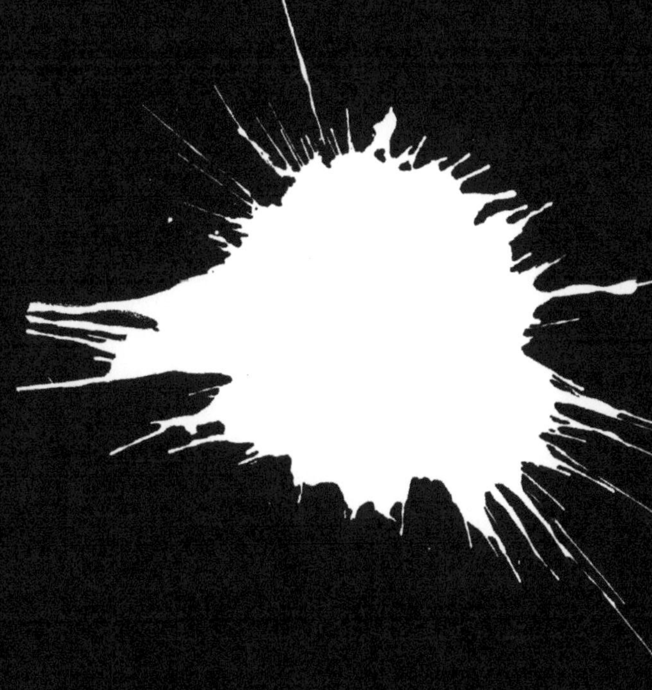

Liars
and
pedophiles
and
beers . . .

Oh, my!

Liars
and
pedophiles
and
beers . . .

Oh, my!

Liars
and

pedophiles
and
beers . . .

Oh, my!

"I don't think we're in Massachusetts anymore."

Umm . . . yes, we are . . . don't lie . . .
silly Motherfuckers.
Nice try!

If you're at all offended
by somethin' that you've read,
just think 'bout how I was feelin'
when I wrote that shit—instead.

Think 'bout how I'm beyond
strenuously tryin' to rid myself
of all of this negativity—inside my head.
And that negative shit . . .

ALL O' FUCKIN' IT . . .

Couldn't possibly have come out said . . .
smellin' like g'damn roses—UNLESS . . .
they were, rigor mortis-ly, fuckin' dead.

I'm overly traumatized—not obsessed,
like they were with their seed—that shit's incest.
This whole fuckin' tree—these perverts infest.

I'm sayin' . . .
how much time "fondlin' penises"
did that other piece o' shit invest!?

Yeah . . .
y'know what . . .

fuck whomever I offend.
I've reached my wit's end.

both middle fingers extend

THERE Y'GO MY FRIEND!

. . . and I use that term fuckin' loosely.
Like their hands in the medicine cabinets—abusely?

Err . . . abusively!

Like the way they'd drunkenly beat his ass—intrusively.

Never knew when to stop—inexcusably!

The amount of time they spent drinkin'—exclusively,
while avoidin' their life, as well as others—reclusively,
has got me talkin' so fuckin' obtrusively . . .

'bout all this shit that's dwelled in my mind—allusively.
But the only thing that helps—is writin' conducively.

I know.
I know.
How obtrusive me.

Fuck this shitty brick road I've most traveled.
I'm fuckin' over it!
Conclusively.

CHOKE ON THIS

I'm startin' to get this feelin',
like we've been here before.

A slipper across the ass,
followed by several more.

His back's b'come covered
in big, red, blotchy-lookin' sores.

He quickly dives under the bed (yet AGAIN).

He's back to starin' at
that g'damn door.

That shit really fuckin' hurt.
He knows he can't take much more.

But the worst has
yet to come.

There's one more attack
he's forced to endure.

He really should've
remained hidden.

As they stumble towards him
across the dinin' room floor.

This time, they've really
gotten his goat . . .

"I

can't

breathe!"

That's a direct quote.

It's all he can whisper out
as their hand's clenched tightly
around his throat.

The "man of the house"
may not see the age of eleven

'cause he's slowly approachin' death.

He's barely takin' in
a new breath.

He's not sure how much longer
he . . . has . . . left . . .

What the fuck did he do
to deserve THIS?

Down his leg
stream beads of piss.

He's about to die,
at the hands of drunkenness
. . . this drunken mess
. . . this inebriated, fucked-up, flesh.

The room begins to black out.
He's about to pass out.

Bein' the "man of the house"

isn't as glorious—as it seems.

He can faintly hear their
Blood-curdlin' screams.

"You're goin' to kill him. Please!"

"STOP!
HE CAN'T BREATHE!
PLEASE!"

It's somewhere near this point,
when he abruptly fell down
to his knees.
No longer constricted
by their deathly squeeze.

Out of fear,
from the general vicinity,
one seed flees.

While, his side, another seed
would never leave . . .

What a fucked-up web
these roots continuously weave.

THE KITCHEN AID UPGRADE

What if I could prove
that it's possible
to overcome all of the odds
which they'd physically implant . . .

By evenin' out
an unbalanced playin' field,
when all of the naysayers say
"rome can't."

What if I tried to change
everythin' about whom I am . . .

Stripped myself down,
to the bare minimum,
in an attempt to recreate
a better man.

What if this was all
a miniscule portion
of God's greater plan . . .

to place me in all of these
fucked-up situations,
so I'd begin to understand

that there's a good reason
why (today) I am who I am.

When all is said, 'n done,
I'm hopin' that you'll
better understand

that our lives have always
been about choices . . .
this next scenario goes
hand-in-hand.

As a seed, he was conditioned
to become well-advanced.

So, he made a choice
not t'be defined
by any one circumstance.

He's never been afraid
to take a direct stance.

He had very little time
for colorin' books,
or boxes of crayons.

By the age of ten,
he was already a "man."

Err—by default . . .
"man of the house,"
understand . . .

He was takin' care
of the other seeds,
in the best possible
way that he can.

Even when certain situations
didn't go exactly the way
that he'd planned.

Or did they!?

He learned the hard way
that a top range burner
set on "HIGH HEAT"
is a horrible place to stand.

When he "accidentally" burnt
the rubber sole off of one

of his (brand-new) dollar-bin sneakers,
while steppin' on a top range burner,
that was heatin' up
without any pans.

OOPS!

Like melted pizza cheese,
his "Skippy" sneakers pulled away
from the stove in long, stringy, stretchy strands.

G'damn . . .

There goes ninety-nine cents
worth of kicks.

Granted, they weren't his
first choice—of picks.

But, at that time,
they were all that he had . . .
except for a cardboard cutout,
that he'd won—that day,
in a basketball game,
against an older leaf, that they once had.

He always knew that they'd let him win
'cause weren't anybody—their age,
that bad.

But he needed those sneaks,
to save himself some embarrassment.
So, he was thankfully glad.

Otherwise, his leaves would've
been beyond hella mad,

at least until he made them an offer
that they couldn't refuse.

Fortunately, that cardboard cutout
he'd won was also a coupon,
that could be redeemed
for a pair of British sneakers
that he told them he'd use.

After breakin' to his leaves
his "misfortune" of news,
they headed to Charlie's Surplus,
so that he could peruse.

This is how he calculatively turned
ninety-nine cent Skippys
into a fifty-dollar pair
of basketball shoes.

That's right.
BKs, not Js . . .
no ruse!

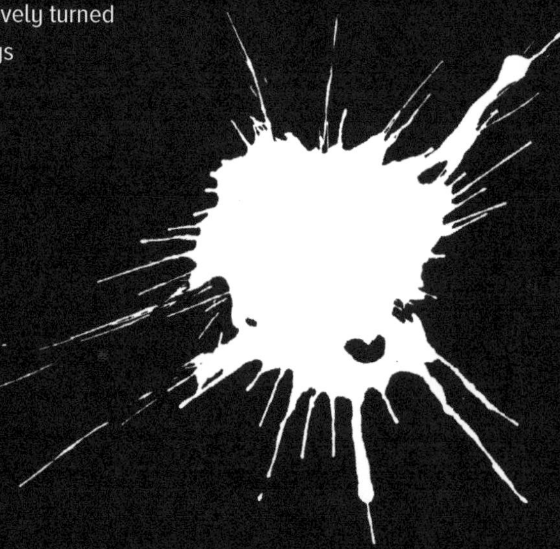

STORAGE WARS

~~MAN OF THE HOUSE~~

Bein' a "latchkey kid"
from the ripe
ol' age of nine,

watchin' over the
younger ones
was his daily job.

After walkin' them home
from school one day . . .
he unlocked the back door
'n quickly found that they
appeared to have been robbed!

While he anxiously began casin'
out the crime scene,
the other seeds stood (in shock)
'n sobbed.

He recalls:
they took the cat,
the food,
the furniture,
AND THEIR FUCKIN' **LEAF**!?

THAT'S TOUGH!

He remembers thinkin' to himself,
"Holy shit!
We've been de**LEAF**ed!"

As if they hadn't already
been through enough.

In a panic,
he began checkin', room to room,
for missin' items
that the robbers
may have muffed.

Like the frickin' house telephone.
Even if he wanted to,
he couldn't call their bluff.

With that said,
his discovery is confusin',
scary, 'n somewhat rough.

Although the robbers took
most everythin'
in the house,
they seem to have
left behind all of
the seeds' stuff?

Empty kitchen.
Empty livin' room.
All of the leaf's shit.
Everything's been jacked.

Empty fridge.
Empty cabinets.
Empty fuckin' coat rack.

Left behind:
one great **BIG**
questionable fact.

When the thieves
emptied out their
entire apartment,
from end to end
(front to back) . . .

THEIR belongings—
were the only things
left behind,
'n intact!?

He wished he'd gotten there sooner,

to catch them in the act.

Another leaf arrived
shortly thereafter,
'n began to unpack.

Good thing, too,
'cause they're gonna need the key
to their storage, in order to get
themselves on track.

Welcome back!

OLIVE BRANCH OF COURAGE

If you've ever been beaten . . .
If you've ever been bullied . . .
If you've ever been assaulted . . .
I can relate to you fully.

Tapped, yet unrooted is ME . . .

"I'M TAPPED"

'n so are YOU,
as well as HE.

You see,
many times I've been told
that I should love life–but I haven't
always been "IN LOVE" with it.

I guess that's the bottom line,
when push comes to shove with it.

. . . And push comes to shove
with it—a lot—no shit.

We've obviously been
through a ton o' shit . . .
done seen a ton o' shit . . .
'n everythin' in between a ton o' shit . . .

yet,
I've never been the one to quit.
Even when I've been
pretty much done with this shit.

I mean, there will be
a couple half-hearted
attempts out of a
self-pity-esque "dummy" fit.

Err . . . "dumb me" fit,
on some stupid shit.

Although,
I won't come remotely
close to full-on endin' it.

I can be dumb,
but I'm not **THAT** stupid—shit.

And, with all that said,
I'm certainly not
recommendin' it.

IF NOTHIN' ELSE,
I'll raise some awareness . . .
"To whom it may concern" with it.

As you can probably already tell,
there's been many sleepless nights.

Both for obvious reasons . . .
and those that the darkness
will persistently entice.

Like, right now . . .
their apartment's over-infested
by roaches, 'n several tiny mice.
And you don't have to tell him twice.
He's NOT shuttin' off those frickin' lights.

It's not happenin'.

But . . .
what IS happenin' . . .
is some bully-slappin' 'n . . .
we'll give you all of **THOSE** deets

which have produced
another sleepless night
beneath his sheets.

As he'll be up 'til dawn,
thinkin' 'bout the days
events—that'd transpired.

He knows he should be sleepin'.
Yet, this adrenaline's keepin'
him from bein' tired.

The slap that shook his jaw.
Man, jus' the sound of it's
still got him wired!

His "leaf's" fearlessness
is a quality he's always desired.

Okay, they're a friend of the tree,
(who's not that much older than he)
whom they've adopted as a leaf.
And if he ever needed a body guard,
NO QUESTION—they're frickin' hired.

Especially t'day.

As he's leavin' the House of Friendliness,
he's encountered by a group
of older kids . . .
(all of whom he knows—
so he thinks he's okay).

When one's homophobic actions
would be put on full display
at his unwillingly subjected expense.

As one unexpectedly grabs him from behind,
'n simulates an act of sex—to his dismay,
he quickly becomes totally tense.

"You like that, faggot!?"
Showin' off, no doubt, for all of his friends.

I guess he was easy prey.
But, he's far from bein' gay
. . . and after all that he's already been through,
the embarrassment is immense.

He quickly runs home, while somewhat cryin',
from this inexcusable event.

Upon explainin' what had happened,
to his leaf, 'n his "leaf" . . .
right back down the street they all went.
And he quickly learned what the sayin'
"It's not the size of the dog in the fight,
but the fight in the dog" really meant.

"Which one?" they inquire.
He hesitantly points—
towards those that conspired.

Then, his "leaf" walked right into the group.
Straight up to his bully . . .

"You think you're tough!?"
"You wanna try that shit with me!?"

SMACK

NO warnin' . . . no response . . . shots fired!

Without hesitation he turned
to the biggest guy in the group:
"You want one, too!?"
He shook his head—no desire.

Then, rather briskly, towards home . . .
the three of them retired.

To this very day . . .
his "leaf" has been someone
whose loyalty, 'n protective nature,
he's wholeheartedly admired!

For havin' his back—
when they weren't required.

Thank you, S.B.!

It meant everythin' . . .

VISUALLY IMPAIRED

I know I said "don't get me started,"
but this shit's just gotta be said.

I couldn't release this shit
with a clear conscience,
havin' left this knowledge
inside my head.

I could've taken this thought
one of many directions.
But I'ma go this route instead.

Please, don't get it twisted . . .
I don't want you t'be misled.

This is about biggest hang up(s).
Pun intended—read ahead.

Growin' up on that branch,
the security of others' belongings
they'd repeatedly breach . . .
by borrowin' anythin' within a hand's reach.

One day, while rummagin' for change,
into that sock drawer they'd sneak.

. . . and, in that sock drawer,
they'd find a nude—of a female freak.

(He could tell by the giddiness
of their reactionary shriek,
that whatever they'd found
was outrageously unique!)

No access to cable channels,
'n they'd already caught a peek.
Which, of course, this little treasure—
they'd immediately leak.
'Cause that's what some of us do—
tongue in cheek.
His thoughts—I imagine,
you probably already know.
But I'll do my best,
to give you a visual—
blow by blow.

Here we go—nice 'n slow . . .

so . . . you know we can't share
the name of this hairy ho,
with a mid-range, out-of-
control, pubic 'fro.

Which kinda confused him—
you should know.

'Cause he didn't know
that hair could grow
around a camel's toe!?

Then again, this was his
first encounter—
with a naked doe . . .
deer . . .
camel . . .

HO!

And since his woolly mammoth
lacked wool—fo'sho!—
he'd never really imagined that area
you'd need to mow.

He's a seed.
What the heck would he know!?

Then it happened.
He gazed up beyond the gap'n
his eyelids, immediately, stopped clappin'.

He's frozen—like a deer in Hooters . . .
milk shooters . . .
red lights . . .
I mean, *headlights*!

Like a deer—in frickin' HEADLIGHTS!
Huge, GINORMOUS, headlights . . .
with medium, round, pink high beams.

Well, right now, low beams.
Heck, you know what I means!

BOOBIES 'n NIPPLES!

The subjects of many adolescent dreams.
The prequel to many prepubescent streams.

The reason he'd often lose vision.
The reason for the forthcomin' decision.
The reason they coined the phrase

"boobie blinded."

****Side note****

As he matured, he'd more frequently
become "boobie blinded."

Sometimes his friends would
have him put his hand in the air
'n cover a female's face—
just t'be reminded.

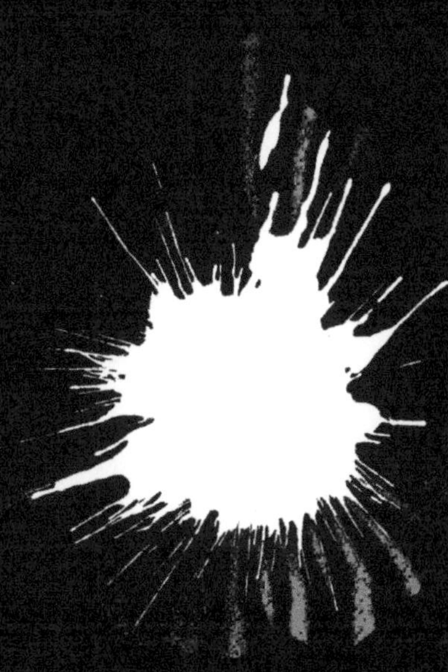

(If you've ever seen him do this,
'n say somethin' like,
"Damn, I wish this sun had subsided!"
Truth be told . . .
your "boobs to looks ratio"
was probably bein' decided . . .
well, at least he was kind/clever
enough to hide it.)

I mean, he had t'be sure
he wasn't just bein' distracted
by a pair of assets
to which he may have become attracted.

He'd later apologize for the way
that he might've acted.

But, for those of you ladies
that are readin' this,
thinkin' that bein' "boobie blinded"
is a myth—that never really existed,

think back to the last time you bragged
to your friends about how you used your
"girls" to avoid gettin' a ticket . . .
because "the twins" just couldn't be resisted.

I just want YOU t'be reminded,
that your officer was probably "boobie blinded"

End side note

just like he was, by her nude picture.

Where it all started . . .
with that hidden gem
of a sock-drawer fixture.

HEROIC

Now that they're old enough
to speak without the fear of
teethin' on bars of soap . . .

I'ma use some fuckin' curse words,
while helpin' them remember
all of the shit, 'n asshole-ness,
that some of their leaves say
that they don't . . .

They're the types to
sugarcoat the past,
'n tell you that everythin'
was "SUPER GREAT!"

That all o' these memories
that we reluctantly "celebrate"
wore a tight blue costume,
that dawned a BIG "S"
(across the chest),
with a flowin' red cape.

While I'm the type to wipe
all of that glucose away,
'n give it to you straight.

Strip it down to the truth
about how adult presence
(when they needed it the most)
has flooded my mind,
with all these fucked-up
memories that I still hate
to this date.

Here's some honesty:
real talk . . .
quite simple,
'n plain . . .

I've become completely
'n utterly ashamed
of their "secret identities"
since, around outsiders,
they don't act the same.

They really need to remain
in their Lowest Lane.

I mean . . .
it's amazin' how much they
pretend to have forgotten.
Believin' all that kryptonite
must be seriously affectin'
their brains.

"Where did I go wrong,
with those seeds?"

It's frequently asked,
yet the question still remains.

And a great fuckin' question
it's been—to pine.

Okay, fine!

I'll give you their example,
alright!?

How about leavin' those
small seeds,
home alone,
into the darkness
of the night.

Alone in the dark,
huddled together,
in the front window,
out of fright.

All of them—scared.
Tellin' themselves,
"Everything's gonna be alright . . ."

Night.
After night.
After night.

Well, five nights a week . . .
but who's countin', right?

As they watched the cars pass by,
hopin' that you just might
come home a li'l bit early,

on that particular night.

"I see a headlight!"
. . . after headlights
. . . after headlights
. . . after headlights.

And on one of those nights,
they pulled the string down
on the blinds, too tight,

which came crashin' off
of the window sill,
'n slightly messed up
one's eyesight.

A nice li'l gash
above their eye.
But you've also forgotten about that.

Am I right!?

Don't sweat it.
I'll continue rememberin'—for them.
I've got this knack for
verbally reconstructin'
the scenes of plight.

This is where one wet a face cloth,
'n applied it to the gash.

Then they sat there,
even more petrified.

'Cause now they're expectin'
that you'll be mad,

‘n probably wanna whoop some ass.

But there was nothin’ that
they could’ve possibly done.

It all happened so frickin’ fast!

They just wanted to watch
for your arrival.

Out the darkness
of the window.
Through the glass.

Maybe THAT’S where
you went wrong,
with those seeds . . .
alas!?

Or, maybe not . . .

no worries.

I’ll keep thinkin’ back.
I’m positive we’ll find
an answer—that’s facts.

Egads!

. . . the fuck did they go wrong
with those seeds?

Someone, please, answer them that.
No, don’t.

ONE RULE

Growin' up in the hood,
there was only ONE rule
'bout gettin' into a fight.

They said:
"If you get into a fight,
you'd better not lose—alright!?

'Cause, when you get back . . .
boy, you'll be in for the fight
of your life!"

Somethin' 'bout this advice
didn't seem at all right.

But who is he to question,
'n cause himself any
unwanted strife.

Fast forward to the seventh grade,

where he was introduced
to gang violence,
at an extremely volatile height.

From underneath a lunchroom table.
Don't judge him—that shit's impolite.

This fight between two sets of "ethnic gangs"
is 'bout to REALLY ignite . . .
'n he may—or may not—
be cowerin' in fright.

Why did he become a high school
"legendary track star,"
as described by a former coach,
regardin' a 100-meter race highlight?

'Cause his "sprint all the way home" game
was hella fuckin' tight!
We're not talkin' 'bout a quick dash.
We're talkin' several miles—
of a left 'n a right.

Now he wasn't runnin'
'cause he enjoyed it . . .

no, don't get it twisted, alright.

He was runnin'—for his life
'cause he was born of the pigment
WHITE!

W-H-I-T-E: spelled with certainty.
Yes, you read that right.
He's not about discrimination.
But . . .
this was, in fact,
his plight.

Truth be told . . .

there were several different gangs
that didn't friggin' care
that he'd meant them no harm.

That also didn't stop them
from jumpin' his friend—with a bat—
while they were all alone

'n ONE HUNDRED PERCENT unarmed.

Shit . . .
his seventh-period (failing) grade
should've sounded an academic alarm.

While everyone else was listenin' in class,
he was plottin' his escape—home,
from this predatory farm.

And . . .
one day . . .
behind them . . .
the door that they'd just exited LOCKED.

His closest seedhood friend,
'n himself, were caught.

So, what do they do?

Fuck it . . .
BACK TO BACK—and fought.
TWO VERSUS SEVEN—they brought.

Now he's swingin' in bunches,
with everythin' that he's got.
But he's wearin' these big,
padded, winter gloves
that a leaf had bought.

I mean, it's fuckin' cold outside . . .
'n his nose is gushin' out snot.

(In hindsight,
he should've removed 'em on the spot.
Really smart . . . NOT!)

'Cause their faces are absorbin'
every single (cushioned) shot . . .

As he'd blot . . .
blot, blot, blot . . .
blot, blot . . .

This was the HARDEST
that he'd EVER fuckin' fought.

'Til that teacher pulled up to the curb,
'n yelled:
"Get in the car!" all distraught.

And brought a screechin' halt,
to this brutal onslaught.

No hard feelings, though.
That's jus' life in Wor-Town, 'n whatnot . . .

PEACE, LOVE, 'n EQUALITY, to ALL!

BIG TOP, BIGGER ISSUES

There are so many
different circumstances,
that fuck me up–deep down inside.

If I'm gonna bare it all . . .
within you, I will confide.

From his originals—he could run.
But from my mind—he cannot hide.

I know the difference
between wrong 'n right.

But I have a tendency
to walk that thin, fine line

from the thoughts on my mind,
to the ones that I write.

Most people run away,
to pursue the circus life.

But this leaf ran away
from the Big Top,
replaced the seeds,
'n his (crazy-ass) wife.

He became a "cheese head."
Leavin' THIS family
in a critical bind.

Now I'm fightin' his struggle,
the one that HE fuckin' left behind.

My life's been one, long-ass tightrope.
I'm always teeterin'—from side to side.

You could fill a clown car
with every time that I've lied,
put on a brave face,
'n said, *"No worries, I'll be fine."*

You don't grow up normal,
with a Barnum 'n Bailey
life like mine.

Everyone's got their own set of issues,
from which they'd paint their faces
just to hide.

Abuse runs rampant amongst us.
It discriminates on neither side.

If I made a short list,
it would go somethin' like this:

Alcohol,
emotional,
sexual,
'n herbal.

Physical,
mental,
psychological,
'n verbal.

I've been through it all.
This shit's NOT fuckin' right!

Unfortunately this IS my circus . . .

I just wish some of these
side show freaks,
WEREN'T MINE!

"No worries, I'll be jus' fine!"

UNFORGIVABLE

This might just be

the most apologetic thought
that I ever attempt to write.

I've got to let it out . . .
'n on this darkness shed some light

on when we were all small seeds.
At the time, we're talkin' post-cockfight.

Damn . . .

Writin' this thought,
I can barely see the page.

Everything's a blur.
Tears streamin'
down my saddened face.

My body's in a tremble.
I can't stop the sobbin',
nor these shakes.

I'm at a loss for words.
Yet, I have so much
I feel like I need to say.

I could never ever pretend
that I understand
your disdain.

I wish that I could clear your mind,
'n alleviate all of your pain.

There's not a day that passes,
that I don't hold myself to blame.

It was my job to protect everyone.
I tried to make sure that nobody
was led astray.

Yes, I hold myself responsible.

I was supposed to keep all of
you out of harm's way.

And (all these years)
I really thought that I had.

I thought that I'd done
what I needed t'do,
to deflect everyone
from anythin' bad.

You have to know that
I'd have given up my life,
just to take each place.

I thought that I'd taken each place.
I thought I'd been the savin' grace.

When they left—without a trace—
how could I not have seen
the look of fear upon each face?

Why wasn't I told sooner?
Why am I only findin' out details now?
As an adult, this way . . .
in the wake . . .

my mistake?

I DIDN'T HEAR ANY OF THE CRIES.

I NEVER HEARD MY NAME CALLED,
FOR CHRIST'S SAKE.
HOW THE FUCK COULD I REMAIN ASLEEP?

Dear God,
WHY DIDN'T YOU HAVE ME WAKE?

Right now, I'm feelin'
extremely let down by myself,
'n it's made me so unbearably sad.

Why in the fuck would anyone
leave seeds in a home alone,
with an elderly "nutcase"
(as they'd often say)?
She treated everyone so fuckin' bad.

And why the fuck
did she bring Satan with her,
to target younger prey?

It makes me so steamin' fuckin' MAD!

If I had known then,
what I know now . . .

I'd have put them into an early grave.
I'd have given it EVERY FUCKIN' THING I had.

In a black body bag,
with a toe tag
that bore their leaf's maiden name.

That fuckin' demented coward,
would have met a permanent
fate—that day.

The day that they screamed,
all the way down the street,
when the "Boogie Ma'am"
finally forced them t'go away.

"If you tell, I'll fuckin' kill you!"

I always thought that threat
was aimed MY WAY . . .

I wear a scarlet letter,
on my heart,
that I don't openly display.

No one knows that it exists . . .
'til today.

A letter that could never,
in a million years,
be taken away.

This is the burden that
I carry with me . . .
EACH 'n EVERY fuckin' day.

To you all, I'm forever sorry . . .
On everythin' I love,
I'm so, so sorry!

For forgiveness,
of my failed efforts
to keep our entire tree safe . . .
I'ma always pray.

We didn't deserve it . . .
Through these eyes

fully filled with tears,
that's really all that,
for now, I can think to say.

RITUALISTIC

I've toed the line,
of clearly thinkin', you see.

As I stand smack-dab
in the middle
of my tree.

Both sides are clearly beggin'
for my undivided attention.
I've begun to separate myself
'n break free.

I no longer have the time
to entertain the dissension.
Lately, some have started
questionin' my loyalty.

But fuck if I have the time
t'be loyal to anyone that's
been unloyal to ME.

Those that are
have been few
'n fuckin' far between.

Yet, if there's one thing
that's always been loyal
in my fucked-up life,

it's my over-demandin' OCD.

That motherfucker's been
"ride or die"
since I was a pimple-faced preteen.

There have been times
when I've had a hold of
my OCD.

And

there have been times
when OCD has had a
stranglehold—on me.

Sometimes I'm able
to control it successfully.

While, other times, I'm compelled
to allow whatever is meant t'be,
just be.

Left, right, both

is a mental combination
that serves as a skeletal key

to unlock the pent-up stress
that prolongs my anxiety.

Left, right, both

is the specific code
that aids in allowin'
my mind to feel

somewhat free.

As free as one can
obsessively
compulsively
be . . .

that is,
without actin' out . . .
disorderly.

'Cause
orderly is the only way
that I maintain a
stable level of sanity.

"Everythin' has a place,
'n there's a place for everythin'"
is my everyday creed.

Whether it's in the
cluster-fucked life,
that I lead . . .

or trapped,
inside of my head,
just waitin' t'be freed.

Left, right, both

Whenever I see
my favorite number . . .
thirty-three.

No matter how many times
I see it—I can guarantee.

Left, right, both

Every single fuckin' time
I drive past the POLAR BEAR,
inflated atop the roof of
that damn Polar Beverage Company.

Left, right, both

Whenever I see
that sign to the city
that single-handedly raised
my siblings 'n me.

Welcome To Worcester
(508)—my forever home—I respectfully,
wholeheartedly, praise thee!

Left, right, both

In those moments when
my brain feels numb,
as I embrace an old memory.
(•EVERY•SINGLE•TIME• confidently)

Left, right, both

is the pattern
in which I blink my eyes,
subsequently.

Hold up!

You thought I was winkin' at you!?
Haha—"My B!"

That's jus' a small portion
of my daily rituals
with the monotonous OCD.

RIDDLE ME THIS

How do we explain normal
to our seeds that can see
all that's beyond funked up
within our dysfunctional tree?

Is it too much to ask
for a tad bit of normalcy?

So that our seeds can see normal
from someone other than just her—
or me?

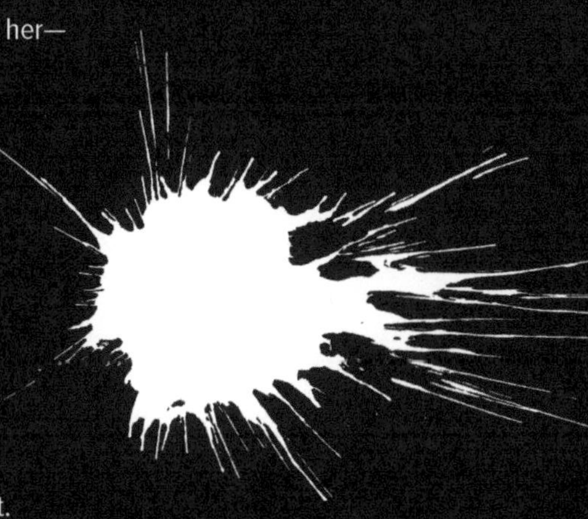

LOST 'N FOUND

It's been tough
knowin' that you're alive,
yet we've never met.

I guess I could've reached out.

Who knows if that's somethin',
later in life,
that I might regret.

But they said they once asked you
why the TWO OF YOU never talked,

'n your response was:
"I didn't think you'd listen."

Now they say that
reachin' out—to you
is a LOST cause.

I can kinda understand
their predisposition.

It must've been a
difficult transition.

I guess I don't know
what I'd do, or say,
if I ever FOUND myself
in your position.

I tend to sit 'n think—A LOT,
'n still can't wrap my head around
your decision.

I just couldn't picture myself
packin' up 'n leavin'.

I fully understand
that she was a nutcase
of a psychotic demon . . .

but to abandon your seeds?
That's not a good enough
fuckin' reason.

I now better understand
their grievin'.

It's true that I've lashed out
at you—many times,
in bitter angst.

You're probably askin' yourself,
"How can he hold
so much animosity
towards someone
he's never met
face-to-face?"

The answer is:
on numerous occasions,
I've mentally sat back
'n TRIED to put myself
in your place.

My OCD has always got me
[obsessively]
[compulsively]
[disorderly]
stressin' over all of the
time that I repetitively waste.

Fast forward,
then rewind . . .
over 'n over.
Play by play.

Mornin',
noon,
'n
night.

Day after g'damn day . . .
in my mind,

I've monotonously pressed "replay."

I still can't figure out
why you chose
t'go out
in such a coward-esque way . . .

I'm sayin', though:
Who tries to
burn a house down
with their seeds runnin' around
inside of the home—anyway?

I really hate to admit it.
But, they're probably
better off that
you didn't choose to stay.

Gone
but not
forgotten.

Just another back-of-the-
milk-carton runaway . . .

LADRÓN

When I first started redirectin'
these thoughts—I was angry . . .

confused . . .
somewhat blind . . .

All of my stress-filled moments,

I'd kept them thoroughly confined.

If I don't think them,
then they don't exist.

So I buried them,
as deep as I possibly could,
within the back of my mind.

That burden belonged to me.
The discomfort I felt—was all mine.

I'm supposed t'be the strong one.
I'm one of the oldest.
I'm expected to always be fine.

I have t'be brave,
for all of us—all of the time.

Somewhere within this outpourin',
the bravest me will be defined.

I've been takin' my frustrations
out on my tree—'n anyone else
I felt was out of line,
while waitin' in line,
to cross that thin line,
of attackin' my integrity.

Those people haven't been
that difficult to find.

When you shake down
my fuckin' tree,
you get a good mixture
of nuts 'n fruits—combined.

Maybe I'm jus' bein' unkind.

Not t'be confused with the masculine,
Spanish pronunciation *el* . . .
No, wait . . . that's not right, let's rewind.
My *español*'s a li'l rusty.

What's the correct word,
that I'm tryin' to find?

I got it!
I'm sayin' that I'm bein'
a fuckin' asshole!

Like their gold-diggin' seed,
who stood by that penny-pinchin' loser.
Leavin' me 'n mine
in a monetary bind.

FUCK THEM . . .
and THEM.

And anyone else
that would knowingly fuck over
their own flesh 'n blood.

For you,
I no longer
make time.

Adiós!

BREAK A LEG

Telephone chat,
‘n telephone chit.

ring•ring•ring

[Incomin’ bullshit]

When it comes to spreadin’ bad news
‘n the latest gossip,

you need not look any farther.
‘Cause this one’s always got that shit.

Their number appears
on your caller ID list.

Followed instantly—by that pit,
that causes an enraged
stomach’s ultimate fit.

As fate would have it,
“relationship,”
to them, always means
“relay some shit” . . .

not jus’ a li’l bit,
but all of its shit.

About you,
about me,
about her,
about him.

Fuck it.
Who the hell am I kiddin'?

"Relationship,"
to them, means "to
relay some shit . . .
to anyone that will
LISTEN!"

It isn't normally full truths.
Most of the facts
will be (purposely) missin'.

Hell,
it may not even be the full story.
They've never been THAT accurate.

'Cause they love to over-embellish.
They get off on this "actor" shit.

They've always had a flare
for the dramatic.
They play the lead role,
like it's some Caster bit.

Welcome to the world premier
of their one-person,
tidbits-of-bullshit skit.

Which starts off with
the ringin' of a phone.
The front screen fully lit.

Yo! Here we go . . .
it's bad news, again . . .
"You might need to sit . . ."

cue the curtain*

GO AHEAD . . .
ANSWER IT!

PLAYAS GON' PLAY

I live by myself,
all alone—
in a mental state
of nonconformity.

Population of ONE!

There's nobody in here,
but me.

No one livin' in my mind,
but me.

This is where I exfoliate
my entire tree.

I flip the flight cap
to the back,
throw on a pair o' Js
that match . . .
'n a dry-fit Jordan tee.

White, red, 'n black, with
my silhouette on the back.
Bold letterin' that reads:
R O M E 3 3.

Now, it's time to get down
to the nitty-gritty.

Before all is said 'n done,
there will be no more
fuckin' wit me.

I'ma make sure that
THAT bridge
has been **BEYOND**
fuckin' torched.

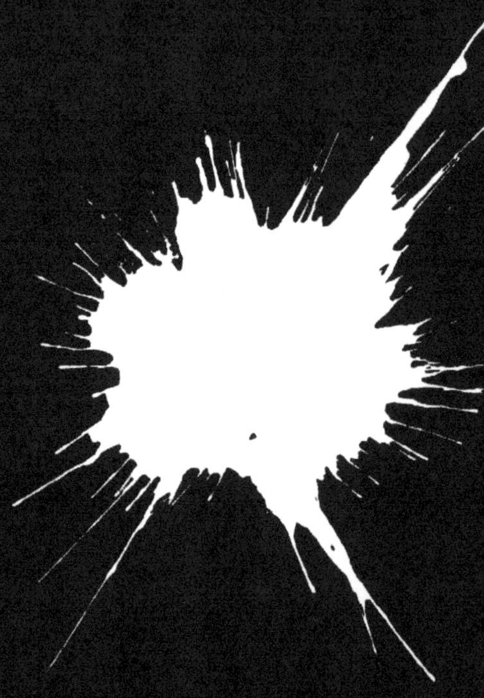

Then, I'm headed into
hibernation.
A retirement, of sorts.

I've grown tired of the
competition.
I'm done sweatin' those
salty, sore sports!

I'm on a spiritual cleanse.
Kinda steppin' up my
nutrition.

While they're takin' their time,
sippin' on haterade,
quart after quarts.

I guess this is where
I publicly thank
some members of my tree,
for their inspiration . . .
off of the basketball courts.

Without their hate,

I'd not have found love . . .
for poetically defecatin'
in each o' their "undershorts."
He squats, he scores!

I LEARNED IT BY COPYIN' YOU

The longest essays
that they've ever written,
had nothin' t'do
with homework,
or book reports,
or even anythin' t'do
with their schools.

In fact . . .
they were written
right AFTER they exited the bus.

When they'd broken one
of the multitude
of household rules.

Yep.
You guessed it.
Too big for spankings . . .
(yet, there's still discipline galore.)

They've begun WRITIN' their punishments,
'til their hands go numb 'n sore.

But, they'll still be forced to finish,
every single assignment—for sure.

For—waitin' for them,
on the kitchen table
when they arrive home,
will be at least FIVE
blank pages (or more).

With a single line written
across the top,
for them to "NEATLY COPY" . . .
you can rest assured.

Every single line.
Front 'n back . . .
is the task they'd be forced
to endure.

No matter how fuckin' stupid . . . or "arbitrary."
Like failin' to finish a single chore.

Write . . . write . . . write . . . write . . . write . . .
in all CAPS, 'til they can't write any more.

While cleanin' up one day,
they'd forgotten to pick up their socks
off of the bedroom floor.

I WILL REMEMBER TO PICK UP MY SOCKS OKAY.

When they left the house, for school,
they accidentally slammed the door?

I WILL NOT SLAM THE DOOR TO THE KITCHEN OKAY.

They were asked a question, but responded
with the wrong "tone of voice" . . .

I WILL BE RESPECTFUL TO ADULTS AT ALL TIMES OKAY.

They fell asleep with the television on,
'n woke up to a rainbow—on the screen,
makin' a beepin' noise.

I WILL TURN OFF MY TV BEFORE I GO TO BED OKAY.

Didn't clean all of the bird shit
out of the cage,
'n off of the adjacent wall.

I WILL TAKE BETTER CARE OF OUR PETS OKAY.

Left their ball layin' around,
which "caused them to trip,"
'n almost fall—in the back hall.

I WILL PUT MY THINGS AWAY WHEN I AM DONE OKAY.

Got home a little late,
from bein' out one day.

I WILL BE HOME IN TIME TO DO MY CHORES OKAY.

Apparently they got the last word in,
'n need to watch what they say.

I WILL NOT TALK BACK TO ANY AND ALL ADULTS OKAY.

It didn't take very long before
their punishments started to feel
out of line—or, if you will, ASININE.

I WILL NOT TOUCH ANYTHIN' THAT ISN'T MINE OKAY.

I WILL NOT SIT IN THE CHAIR AND RECLINE OKAY.

I WILL NOT BE IN THE WRONG PLACE AT THE WRONG TIME OKAY.

. . .'n so on,
. . . and so forth,
. . . 'n et cetera.

With this type of shit—I could go on 'n on.
I've got a plethora.

But each 'n every one ends
with their utter dismay.

Hell,
if they could punish **ME** today,
I can just imagine what **THAT** shit would say . . .

I WILL NOT WRITE MEMORY BOOKS ABOUT OUR TREE OKAY.

OLIVE BRANCH TO COPE

I've lost my will—to live
more times
than I could ever count.

It's a good thing—for me
that my fear of dyin' . . .
nothin' in life—could ever surmount.

This might seem kinda strange.
But I don't deal very well with change.
As, by now, you've already seen.

My OCD prefers everythin'
in my life in a specific order—pristine.

Followin' the pattern
of my day-to-day routine.

Maybe that's not as odd,
as I make it out—to seem!?

I mean . . .

I'm sure, if I Google it,
I could find an "OCD MEME."

Possibly an image
of a noose-tied rope,
held by a young boy—strugglin' to cope.

With a caption across it
that reads,

"Never succumb to an obstacle
that tries to intervene between
YOU 'n YOUR wildest dreams."

Right now,
change is that noose.

But many miles away,
is where I'd like to discuss
a new outlet—for this recluse.

Upon movin' to "the sticks"
from the streets . . .

it happened—once again,

within a new friend,
that he was fortunate enough to meet.

God introduced him—to a female
whose confidence was
above 'n beyond elite.

She was pretty,
liked walks,
'n reminded him (a lot) of D.T.

And—yet again . . .
(most importantly)
when no one else did,
she gave him the attention,
that he'd inevitably need.

Whenever she'd call,
he knew exactly what she'd say:
"Do you wanna go for a walk?"

Then they'd meet up half-way.
Behind the old elementary school,
that's where they'd go—to talk.
Nearly every day.

On the swings,
they'd laugh 'n conversate . . .
for hours at a time they'd stay.

Just himself 'n J.M.
(To this day, he affectionately calls her "J.")

Much like his friend "D" . . .
she has this calmin' sorta way,
of speakin' to him with care

'n takin' all of his anguish away.

That type of tenderness
(towards a "stranger")
is extremely rare—this age and day.

She's become another life-long friend.
Despite their schedules, 'n distance,
since the military moved her away.

Forever in debt—to her friendship.
Without it, there's no tellin'
where he might be today.

INCARCERATION

He's always gotta have
the last word.

Otherwise, he doesn't feel
like he's been properly heard.

I know this may sound a bit absurd.
But provin' them wrong
is satisfyingly fun—'n preferred

which is probably why
he's yet t'be deterred.

Lately, he spends more time
in his bedroom
than anywhere else in the house.

Not because he enjoys bein' in there.

TAPPED YET UNROOTED

They tell him that it's
"because of his smart mouth."

So, here he is, yet again.
GROUNDED . . .
for • the • entire • summer.

Wanna take one guess as to what it's all about?

We'll wait

This time a healthy communicative exchange
escalated into a shout.

They hate bein' wrong,
which landed him back in a familiar place
for an extensive time out.

They have to stand guard at his door
with strict instructions:
"DO NOT allow him to come out."

pout

They've always been their favorite—NO DOUBT!

Playin' warden for an older seed.
Yeah, I'd say they've got a little more clout.

Yet, for as long as they have his back,
he'll never be forced t'go without.

That is, until the leaves return home—each night.
Then his sentence resumes.

LIGHTS OUT

in cell block E,
for inmate 51773.

ALL JOKIN' ASIDE

He used to look up to that leaf.
They would come second to none.

He'd felt like their favorite seed.
As a leaf, they were his number one.

Any time they spent together,
he considered it t'be fun.

Whether it was just hangin' out
with them around their house,
or runnin' out on a car ride,
for a (quick) store run.

It's amazin' how quickly
relationships can switch lanes.

fast forward through high school
Where everythin' has changed.

New apartment,
new town,
new car,
new life . . .
new strife—shit is strange.

They're no longer that close.
Far away gone—are those days.

Along with the belts,
in which their asses
had (many times)
been firmly grazed.

They've grown out of
those type of punishments.

But, with little room for error,
tempers are quite easily fazed.

He learned that the hard way,
on one of those particular days.

When he "crossed the thin line."
So, in front of his friends—
without any haste,
they smacked him in the mouth—
right across his face.

talk about embarrassing

For sayin' somethin' "in jest,"
they quickly put him back in his place.

Fallin' (awkwardly) backwards,
down the second-floor stairs.
Now his head's in a daze.

He'd ask himself:
"What the fuck was that for!?"

As he's lookin' up to them again,
(this time, from his back)
layin' on that narrow staircase.

If you've ever been struck
by someone you care about,
you know this bitter taste . . .
it forever lingers in your mouth.
When the mutual respect
(that you once shared)
has been replaced.

One time . . .
sometimes that's all it takes.

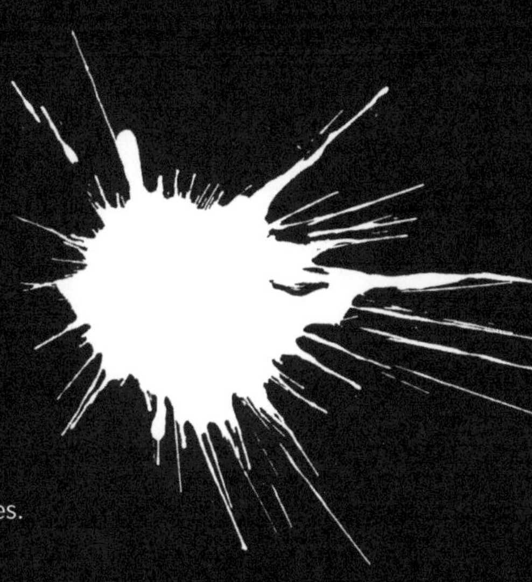

PAR FOR THE COURSE

For far too long,
I've internalized too many issues.

For my swan song,
I've external cries into many tissues.

When did I become
such a danger—to myself?

When did I start placin'
everyone else's opinions
before my health?

They say I've done my share of wrong.
I say I've done my share of right.
They say I've done my share of run.
I say I've done my share of fight.

Through all of the hate,
I still kinda feel like I'm destined
for somethin' great.

TAPPED YET UNROOTED

Even though lately
I've been so casually impatient,
while I hurry up 'n wait.

Someday they'll wish they'd helped me,
through this journey
of unquestionable fate.

When I had no food
but my troubles filled a full plate,
they may have turned their backs on me,
but still they ate off of my volatile state.

It goes without sayin' but:
Haters don't discriminate.

So, fuck 'em!

I know that I'm destined for greatness!
I can feel it in my heart.

No doubt, they'll regret not pitchin' in,
'n playin' (at least) their part.
Instead of kickin' around the pieces,
when I was puzzled—'n fallin' all apart.

Some days I sit
'n think of all the ways
that I could dismantle
that friggin' tree.

Screw every single picture frame
that allows false allegations
t'be spread carefree.

Fuck a crabapple . . .

or a lousy, lying leaf.

Someday I'ma do it.
I'ma suffocate
the ancestral air
that excretes
from within this tree.

While marchin' to my own drum,
through Solo headphone Beats . . .
I'ma walk right straight through,
into the belly of the beast.
That shit doesn't faze me.
Not in the fuckin' least.
I'm Worcester, MA—born 'n raised.
No stranger to those streets . . .
woods . . .

I wish a motherfucker would . . .
question my loyalty.

I'd prop their ass up
on a tee—that's faithful.

Then answer them with a driver,
as I *SMASH* that "loyal tee."

Eighteen holes
should cleanse the soul.
It's time I start
takin' care—of ME.

FORE!

NOW YOU KNOW THEIR BCDs

In case you hadn't noticed . . .
there's a "B" hive that hangs,
lowly, from a branch on the tree.

So long as no one pokes at it,
the happier they'll all be.

Now,
one's always been his ride or die.
He says this rather frequently.

His partner in crime.
His "P.I.C."
But, in this thought, they're jus'
another "D."

He'll forever be their keeper,
that's as real
as real can be.

No one gets to them
without first havin'
t'go through him—desperately.

That is . . .
until that dreaded time,
when they were made
to fly around—separately.

The "Worker Leaf" (King B) decided
to flex those wings,
'n their hive
he was forced to flee.

He saw this shit comin'.
It's been buildin' up—for weeks.

This is just one—of the many times
that he's been stung—on the cheeks.

He's without his yellow jacket.
He was forced to leave
their honeycomb—rapidly.

Which left "D" unguarded
from the torment
of these "B"s.

If you want the
worker's attention . . .
with the queen you must compete.

"D" never stood a chance.
They'd fight, 'n argue—constantly.

Then one day
the game all changed . . .

When a "B" called "D" a
"C" . . . you next Tuesday,
'cause "D" is fast asleep.

They've started takin' medication
to induce a comatose sleep.

Until the worker arrives
back home each night,
the queen won't
hear a peep.

This is what happens
when you choose honey
over waterin' your seeds.

You put forth more effort
into pollinatin' other flowers . . .
than you do protectin' the colony
'n their personal needs.

I call "B"s wax—on anyone that disagrees!

HOMELESS

Yes,
I've been thrown out
of "homes,"
with nowhere t'go . . .

just me 'n my clothes,
kickin' stones
in the road.

On more than
one shitty occasion.

I guess I'm of the
"home invasion"
persuasion?

Since it didn't take
much persuadin'
to kick my adolescent ass
to the curb.

Eviction notices . . .
"Oh . . . YOU GOT SERVED!"

Abandoned, f'real . . .
so fuckin' absurd!

And
and
AND . . .

both situations evolved
around seeded bullshit.

The fuckin' nerve.

Apparently,
I must've twice hit
that same g'damn nerve.

Once with So 'n so.
Once with Such 'n such.
I've observed.

But for two,
totally opposite,
of the spectrum,
reasons.

To the one in particular,
they'll always pledge their
undyin' (often sickenin')
allegiance.

So, it came as no surprise,
that they believed
all of those lies

'n took that freakin' side . . .
OVER MINE.

This shit happens
all the time.

No point in filin'
a relative grievance.

They packed up
everythin' of mine,
into bags of every kind,
whatever they could possibly find . . .
'n threw them all outside.

Like unwanted trash . . .
in a single-file line.

Which was totally
freakin' fine.

They must've had
legitimate reasons.

The fuckin' heathens.

It's not like
bein' shit on
isn't somethin' that
I'm not already
totally used to.

'Cause, on the other side,
there was but one goal.

Which stemmed around

serious issues of full-on control.

That finally took
an ugly toll,
when I sent that
recliner for a stroll.

Okay . . .
Okay . . .

I tossed it clear across
their fuckin' living room,
'n watched that
motherfucker roll.

I could get into
that whole fucked-up ordeal,
but I wholeheartedly refuse to.

PSYCH!

You paid good money
for y'boy rome
to unequivocally amuse you . . .
so, I shall.

Their way
or NO way
is the ONLY way . . .
LEGIT.

We've already established
that outlandishly wack bullshit.

So the long-winded
explanation I'll happily omit.

On this day,
the fan wasn't the only thing
that was gettin' hit with shit.

They'd felt that their blame
was justifiably fit.

Which meant that
there'd be no chance
in freakin' hell
that I would be acquit.

Hold up,
I wasn't wearin' any gloves.
"SHIT!"

So,
kicked back
to the curb—I'd sit.

Now,
I know full well
that two wrongs
certainly don't
make a right . . .

but it sure as hell
makes us even.

Since they decided to throw
the book at me while leavin' . . .
I'm throwin' THIS one back.
Hell, I'll sign them a copy, even . . .

Dear _____ 'n _____,
Thanks for all of

the negative support
that I've recently
been receivin'.

I know you've both had
reasonable doubts.

But here it is.
In spite of everythin'
you've put me through,
I'm above 'n beyond,
achievin' . . .
'n
since you're currently readin' . . .

you can probably, begrudgingly, admit . . .
that seein' is believin'.

Sincerely,
—rome

As written, from **MY OWN HOME**.

The one which I own.

The ONE from which
I've never been thrown.

It's nice to finally have a place
that I'm not scared 'bout bein' forced
into permanently leavin'.

Sad . . . isn't it!?

A LITTLE GOES A LONG WAY

Respect
REspect
RESpect
RESPect
RESPEct
RESPECt
RESPECT
R-E-S-P—YOU KNOW THE REST.

I'm the type of guy
that always shows
respect FIRST.

Then I sit back patiently,
in hopes of bein' reimbursed.

I don't believe in proddin'.
No one should ever
have t'be coerced.

All I ask is for
a little reciprocation.
But with them,
this is the worst.

They've got a different
outlook on respect.

Of which I'm not a fan.

The act of givin'
is the aspect
they tend to neglect.

Yet, from them,
YOUR respect
is ALWAYS in demand.

I'm a consummate gentleman.
Hell, I'm a gentle man.
But, I'm not a fuckin' genie.
You're wishful thinkin'
with that command.

It's time I put this thought
to rest.

I'ma break it down.
As simple as I can.

If you don't GIVE,
you don't fuckin' GET!

I shouldn't have to explain this,
to anyone—understand?

I don't care if you're
younger, or older.
For disrespect, I will not stand . . .

or sit.
Or take it lyin' down.

If the square's your fit . . .
EMBRACE IT!
I'm so tired of fuckin' 'round.

HTF!?

If he were me
And I were him,
I'd be so proud
of where he is now
as opposed to where
he's been.

And I AM.

As for them . . .
how the fuck
are we related?

I've asked myself
this question
a time or two.

How did I turn out
to become like ME?

Growin' up
amongst the likes
of YOU . . .

Hi, my name is . . . *bleh bleh bleh*
You can go to fuckin' hell
'n screw!

I know what you're thinkin' . . .
"rome, that's a little harsh."

I get it . . .
you're right . . .

it's true . . .

hell,
I'd take it a step farther
to say it's downright rude.

But I shouldn't have to
reintroduce myself
to members of the tree
that I can't even remember
the last time
I've spoken to.

Fuck a family feud.

I know who's always got my back
'n they know I've got theirs, too.

When I reached a certain age,
I latched on to a
permanent point of view.

That I would turn out
t'be a great person,
in spite of all that y'all
said . . .
or chose t'do.

That I would become
my own entity,
'n learn from
ALL OF OUR mistakes.

Then try to figure out
my own niche,
in every path

that I chose to take.

Allow me to list a few.

I've never had a sip of alcohol.
I couldn't tell you
how that shit tastes.

I've seen countless nights
of drunken anarchy.

I've a proud appreciation
of my coherent,
sober state.

Since addiction already
runs within our tree,
I chose not to participate
in that race.

I've never tried a drug,
nor smoked anythin'
of the like.

I've always wondered
why some of y'all did them
around that kitchen table,
smokin' them purple trees
in front of us tykes.

Y'all know
THAT shit
wasn't friggin' right.

I'm not gonna get into
all of the other drugs.

That's another addiction
I chose not to fight.

Most importantly, to me . . .
I've never turned a deaf ear
to any of the seeds.
And I've certainly never
turned my back.

A lot of you can't claim
one or the other,
to this bold-faced fact.

Not an addiction,
but still a fuckin' sad
way to act.

To those of you, I say:

Even though we
no longer communicate,
and our relationships
have become informal . . .
I hold on to the memories.

Way back when,
at least some of y'all,
were "somewhat,"
kind of,
a tad,
(dare I say)
a little bit normal.

How the fuck are we related?

No, seriously . . .

ROTTEN TO THE CORE

At times I write so angrily
that even my pen is like:

". . . the FUCK WAS THAT!?"

This is one of those times.
Just so you know exactly
where my head is at.

There are some things
in your life
that you just can't do,
or else you'd cause
your tree great shame.

For instance:
You can't elope
with a cantaloupe.

It tells you that
right in its
frickin' name.

Thankfully,
there aren't any
cantaloupes on my
tree.

Because we'd
(most likely) be
the ones to try.

We've had "relationships"

within our dysfunctional tree
that were disturbingly
NON-consensual.

Well, I should say:
older, predatory seeds
on unsuspectin' younger seeds,
who were forced to comply.

Which brings me back
to them fuckin' apples.

In particular . . .
THAT ONE I once punched,
right in the fuckin' eye.

When it comes to one's
sexual preference,
I make a conscientious effort
to never pry.

I truly believe that there's
someone for everyone.
It doesn't matter, girl or guy.

But that piece of shit,
degenerate
of a rotten fruit,
is absolutely bi.

There's a reason
why that matters,
'n I'ma tell you
PRECISELY why:

I hear they now have

small seeds
of their own.

That thought alone
makes me wanna cry.

"But, rome, what if they've changed?"

"What if" won't replace the past.
"What if" isn't gonna fuckin' fly.

How does this shit
get swept under the rug,
like it doesn't exist?

These innocent seeds didn't deserve
those life-changin' incidents.

They shouldn't have ever
felt that scared.

My eyes are now blurred, 'n tear'd

How could they have known
that "that *bahstid*" was someone
that should've been feared?

Where in the fuck
was a guardian?

Better yet . . .
where was a leaf,
that fuckin' cared?

I could tell you where . . .
but this thought isn't about that.

So . . . it's neither here, nor there . . .

right now, I'm overly concerned
for their seeds.

But no one's ever been willin' to lend an ear.
How many times can life be **THIS** unfair?
No one deserves that kind of fear.

I SCREAM, YOU SCREAM

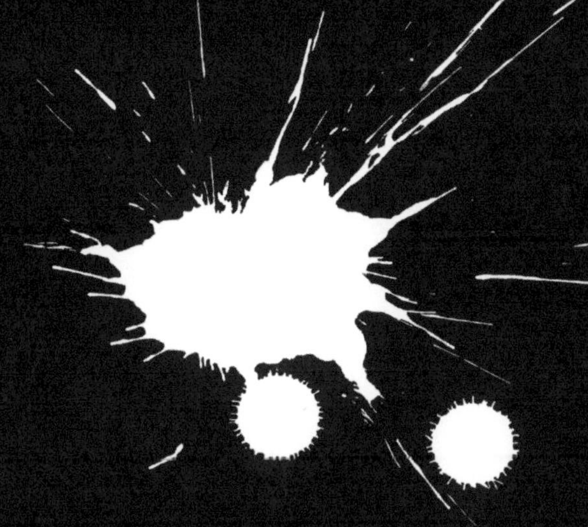

I'm about to start
callin' people out
on all of their
petty bullshit.

If you feel the need
to speak my name,
you'd better not
fuckin' abuse it.

The reasons why I
now keep to myself
are not for your own
personal amusement.

All of the games you play,
'n drama you bring . . .
all of that shit
hinders my self-improvement.

As you sit there
questionin' why I
choose to express myself

this way . . .

while accusin' me of
schemin' ridiculous
plots.

Don't be afraid of the rome
who sits all alone,
writin' those angry,
therapeutic,
thoughts.

If that's the way he
copes with your nonsense,
I'd be more concerned
when his writin'
STOPS . . .

but you've gotta give
y'boy his props.

He shows a li'l bit more restraint,
towards all of your negative plots . . .

than seeds runnin'
down the street,
layin' sneaker rubber
beneath their feet,
as they pound the
ground, on hot concrete,
in the midst
of the summer's
blisterin' heat,
screamin' that catchy
megaphone jingle on repeat,
when that melodious beat

from the ice cream truck's
loud speaker drops.

"Freeze pops!"

They'd better think, before
mentionin' my name.

Take a second to remember,
from whence it came.

Just remain in your lane,
'n I'll do the same.

No one wins
in an altercation
of the name-shamin' game.

HER ADDICTION

The apple didn't
fall far from
her leaves.

Her leaf's a popper,
who deceives
doctor after doctor . . .
in 'n out of prescription pills,
she carelessly,
aggressively
weaves.

We've been subjected
to the epidemic.

Like seeds, like leaves.

Here's my personal gripe:
My tree's no stranger
to the needles,
the pills,
or the pipe.

We've all heard
the term "dope boys."
But I feel the need
to inform you
that "DOPE GIRLS"
are also a type.

They've been around
forever.

Neither's a prototype.

She'll tell you she's been clean,
for such 'n such time.
Don't you,
for a second,
believe the hype.

I can't stand the
"it won't happen to me"
attitude that she's depicted.

If you unwillingly shake,
'til your next fix,
you're **ALREADY** fuckin' addicted!

These drugs keep their
household conflicted.

It's not rocket science, people.

Everyone knows that drug dealers
have specific agendas.
These agendas have been known
to ostracize traumatized lives.
While they vandalize tantalized highs.
There's no discrimination of nose dives.
We need to open our g'damn eyes.

Although, it's not my job
to analyze the lives
of scandalized "wives."
I'm compelled to find solutions
that epitomize compromise,
when it involves certain
members of mines.

They say,
"She's exchangin' 'sexual favors'
for drugs,
in search of higher highs."

But I'd like to believe that
those are just more lies.

Yet, I know I'm just tellin' myself
adorned lies . . .

The shit she's doin'
on those streets.
The shit that's led her
between those sheets.
I can no longer decipher between
fictional 'n factual deets.
She's got a serious problem,

that can be seen through
those bloodshot eyes.

And today
she almost crossed over.
Towards that white light
on the other side.

She didn't hear
the petrified cries . . .
through the door,
from the outside.

Lyin' there,
unresponsive,
from an overdose,
on a bathroom floor . . .
she nearly dies.

But this isn't the last time
she tries . . .

drugs . . .
drugs . . .
'n more g'damn drugs . . .

She's a dope girl,
chasin' those ever-elusive new highs.

GUILTY BY ASSOCIATION

Embarrassment is:
When you show up
at familiar places

‘n receive apologies
from familiar faces,
that have witnessed . . .

first-hand the way
that they were raised,
but felt the need to
“mind their business.”

They say “so many times”
they wanted to help them,
but didn’t want t’be
known as snitches.

NOW
they’re comin’ out in bunches,
professin’ them their well wishes.

[I say “them” because
they’re not the only one (like this)
that they’d end up greetin’.

After all, this is where everyone mingled.
So, to their seed, the same type of spiel
they’d end up repeatin’.]

Talkin’ to them like . . .
We knew how bad it was.
We knew that, at times,
you weren’t (at all) eatin’.

We knew how sad it was.
We knew that, at times,
you were (alcohol) beaten.

We really don’t know how

you made it out alive!
But we're glad that
you're here with us today,
for this meetin' (more or less).

IMAGINE!?

Can you fathom
the type of embarrassment
that they're overcome with in this case?

They'd just shown up, to the spot,
'n they're already feelin'
well out of place.

I mean,
they've literally watched
this book play out—in person.
Gosh, what a frickin' disgrace . . .

let's cut right to the chase.

How many of you have been
greeted in public,
with a guilt-ridden cheek kiss
'n a lukewarm embrace!?

Let alone several.
From tree acquaintances
jus' tryin' to save face.

Sometimes they'd wish that
nothin' was said—but rather
instead that they'd kept it hush.

'Cause it was even harder on their seed.

Yet, they've never been one
to speak out, nor cause a fuss.

The conversations, as a whole,
at times, just became too much.

Showin' up where everyone knows
ALL of your personal business.
THE GOOD, THE BAD,
THE UGLY, etc. 'n such . . .
nah . . . that literally **SUCKS**!

A WORD OF ADVICE

If you've ever told me somethin'
secretive—in confidence . . .

Right now you're probably
frantically readin',
in search of the consequence.

Thinkin':
"Holy shit!
Now rome's got an audience.
He's bound to retaliate,
with somethin' so ominous."

But that's never been
what this process is about.

Revenge isn't gonna clear
my negative thoughts out.

EVERYTHIN' MUST GO!

I'ma yell, scream, 'n shout.

It's a thought clearance SALE.
To which I'm a buck-ten devout.

For the first time in my life,
I'M THE ONE WHO'S SELLIN' OUT!
(Of both thoughts, 'n books.
So . . . break out 'n check out.)

For lack of a better term,
it is what it is—it just fits.

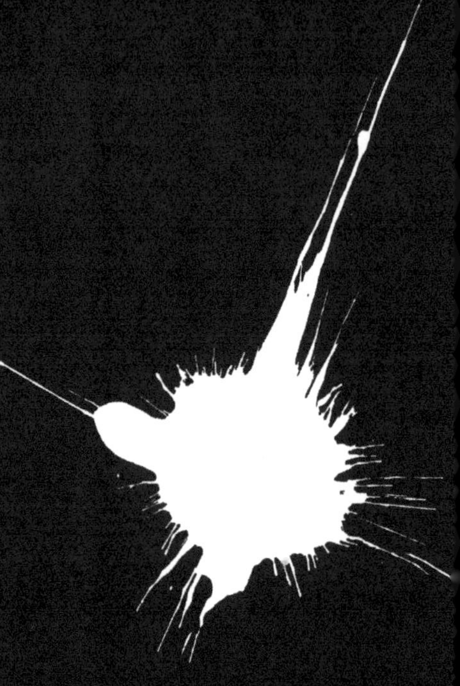

So, where am I keepin'
those secrets which
most of you have entrusted
my poetic ass with?

Locked in my mind.
'Cause y'boy's not a snitch.
(But, I'm also not a gullible twit.)
Yep, that's where all of THAT
juicy, yet informative, material sits.

Unwritten poems—ANOTHER manuscript.
Yes, a Part II.
Entitled "Writin' Fire—rome's Greatest HITS."
Where I tell EVERYONE
EVERYTHIN' you should be glad I omit.
And I mean everythin' . . . think about it.

Waitin' (quietly) on the first person
that gains some confidence
'n gets the notion to pop off
on some ridiculousness.

I'm fully prepared to release the sequel
to this outpourin', bitch!

You know who you are.
So, while you're ahead . . .
let it go—jus' QUIT!

As I emphatically call on myself:

*****BULLSHIT!!*****

Followed by a huge
"PSYCHE!
'CAUSE IT WILL NEVER EXIST!"

There won't be a f'kin' tell-all.
I jus' felt the need to get your
panties all up—in a twist!

You all should've known
that I'm not like that.
Case closed 'n dismissed . . .
you sue-happy motherfuckin' idiots.

SKEPTICAL

I'm a Masshole.
You're jus' an asshole.
There **IS** a significant difference.

I can't stand dealin' with ignorants.
While you've overindulged on ignorance.
See the significance!?

POETIC WORD SLAUGHTER

Lemme ask you . . .

how do you keep it real,
when everyone you know
is hella fraudulent?

How you speak your mind,
when every word of truth
sparks a new argument?

How you remain well-rounded,
when all of the squares turn up
on cue?

I'm sayin' . . .

how you expand your circle,
when you've got trust for
very few?

My vulnerability has been shed.
Since I climbed back inside my head.
Now, lookin' outward on all I dread.
There's that fine line I tend to tread.
All the bullshit I've been force-fed . . .
keeps raisin' doubts upon words said.

"Skepticism"

Nearby, naive negligence non-equivalently
normalizes nonsensical nepotism.

Nuh-nuh-nuh-knowingly . . .

. . . and it sucks.

Not even family can you trust.
Favoritism amongst seeds is unjust.
Y'know, I really hate to cause a fuss.
But . . .
a rebellion is a must . . .
'n I've visibly run out of fucks . . .

. . . to give.

WHAT THE FUCK!?

Can I live!?

Without constantly bein' reminded
about him 'n his . . .

or her . . .

Fuckin' **GRRRRR**

I'm back in a passion-filled mood.
We're constantly rehashin'
this family feud.
What was in that shitstorm
that they brewed?

The one meant to divide the *me*s from *you*s.
No longer influenced by ice-cold brews.
I hate t'be the bearer of bad news.
But there goes their fallback excuse.

And I'm no longer entertainin' abuse.
Physical, sexual, verbal, nor mental . . .
I've paid more than my fair share of dues.

With that, this poem concludes.

Abruptly.
Fuck it.
How rude.
That's not coincidental.

I'm a Masshole.
You're jus' an asshole.
There **IS** a significant difference.

OLIVE BRANCH OF LOVE

My dearest R.M.E.,

There are some things that I tell you,
while others remain untold.
Although I like to save some
of my feelings—for myself.
I'm about to bare my soul.
This might sound a li'l crazy.
But there's somethin' that I want you to know . . .

I knew that I loved you
on our first date.
From the time I picked you up,
'til we had to part ways,
everythin' about that night
had me thinkin': soulmate.
I was so nervous
that I wound up runnin' late.
I even came up with a long explanation,
as to why I made you wait.
But then you walked towards my car,
'n took my breath away.
Along with my explanation.

All I could muster up was a soft-spoken "hey."
As I opened up your door for you.
That smile on your face.
God, you looked so beautiful,
on that cold, snowy day.
Then we bumped into my family at the restaurant,
'n I thought to myself: "Oh, great . . .
This is gonna be awkward."
But when you told me
how good it made you feel,
to see me interact with my niece,
I jokingly told you, "It was fate."
And now I know that it was.

I knew that I loved you
when I first touched your lips.
Butterflies filled my stomach.
A feelin' that I'd missed.
Followed by a sense of fear.
'Cause I'd never felt like this—so quick.
It still brings a smile to my face
every time I reminisce . . .
on the night we went to the movies
but the entire show we missed.
But I still say you made the first move
when it came to that first kiss.

I knew that I loved you
when you turned our house into a home.
It takes a special type of person
to embrace someone else's seeds—as their own.
But you came in 'n made it clear
that we'd no longer be alone,
by the way you embraced us,
with all of the love that you've shown.
We've undergone so many changes.

It's amazin' how, together, you 'n I have grown.
Opposites really do attract.
Isn't that somethin' . . .
who'd have known?

I knew that I loved you,
when I proposed on Christmas Eve.
Your engagement book came out perfect.
But it wouldn't be complete
until I got down on one knee,
placed that ring on your finger,
'n asked you to marry me.
I often think forward to our wedding,
'n how amazin' it'll be . . .
to have 'n to hold.
When you 'n I become "WE."

I knew that I loved you,
when you gave birth to our baby boy.
I cried on that day—down my cheek—tears of joy.

I knew that I loved you,
when I kissed your forehead,
this mornin'—before I went on my way.
Because I never want you to have any doubts.
Those are always the last words that I say.

So that you'll forever be aware that . . .
I knew I loved you . . .

REBEL WITH A CAUSE (PART I)

I wake up every mornin',
'n think of new ways

to set myself apart.

I'm buildin' my own legacy.
Which, to me, is a lost art.

How will I be remembered:
for my finish,
or by my start?

I'ma write my
fuckin' heart out.
I'ma leave nothin'
said in jest.

I'ma pour my heart
onto this paper.

And regardless of what you think . . .
when all is said, 'n done,

I'ma make it certain
that you've read my
absolute very best!

Right now,
I can just imagine
the pale looks on
my tree-frames'
astonished faces.

I envision them
t'be—all the same.

As I've not a doubt
that some of you have
already put a name

to each 'n every
single thought
that I proclaim.

And when, in fact, you did,
like it or not . . .
you also realized that you
had just acknowledged
this shit as bein' **TRUE**.

Because it is—which you
already knew.

Now you're feelin'
beside yourself,
knowin' that you've
already pointed a finger
or two . . .

and one (or more)
of those fingers
that you've pointed
were aimed directly
BACK—AT YOU.

But for those of you
that aren't from the tree,
I'm sure you understand,
that I meant well.

What I write is not a slam
against my tree.
I love them all "just swell."

But I had to clear my conscience.
On all of this mental burden

I could no longer dwell.

It was just a matter of time,
before one of us lost our minds.

Might as well have been ME—
who fuckin' rebels!

PROPS TO YOU (PART II)

By now some of you
are probably thinkin',
"What in the fuck
has this guy been through!?"

While some of you others
are probably thinkin'
that somethin' I wrote
pertains to you.

By now you might be embarrassed,
'cause you jus' found out
that these thoughts,
from my head,
are, in fact, all true.

While some of you others
might be embarrassed
by the visually graphic pictures
that I poetically drew.

By now I bet that some
of you are wishin' that
you could claim yourselves

in a poem . . .
or two.

While some of you others
are more than likely wishin'
that no one points a finger your way.
Once they start puttin' together
two 'n two.

By a show of hands:
how many of you are hidin'
behind an admission of guilt?
I know there are quite a few—of you.

Now, how many of you are wonderin'
which guilty parties raised their hands?
Just sittin' there.
Wonderin' WHO?

By now at least one of you
is wishin' that I'd mentioned your name.
Jus' because you threatened
that if I did, you'd sue.

At this point, some of you
are now thinkin',
"How fuckin' insecure, if that shit's true."

While I'm sittin' here
with the rest of you
thinkin', "What kinda douche
threatens to sue—over said truths?"

But I already knew the answer,
'n I'm sure (by now)
most of y'all do, too.

If not at all by name,
then through my written
point(s) of view.

In any case . . .
much respect for stickin' through!
I'd love to reach out 'n thank y'all—individually.
But, for now, this'll have t'do.

"THANK YOU!"

BLACK SHEEP

I write with a heavy heart,
to get this shit off my chest.

I'm the opposite of lifted.
I guess you could say I'm de-pressed.

My feelings have been worked out so hard.
To recuperate, they'll need extensive rest.

But there's no rest for the restless.
When you attempt to one-up my better,
you inadvertently antagonize my best.

Which, to them, won't really matter.
Because my best is never good enough.
They'll continue to belittle me,
behind my back—in jest.

Insecurity is a lonely feelin'.
I've begun to question my loneliness.

TAPPED YET UNROOTED

Why me?
What do you want?
From where did you manifest?

How can I have these feelings?
Who do I trust?
Are these REALLY my family 'n friends?

When I walk into a crowded room,
I can tell, by the awkwardness,
that their words already got to them.
Each 'n every one of them.
At my expense.

They look at me in such a way
that you'd think that I was there
to rob the place.
I'm waitin' for her to start shufflin'
through her purse in search of her
can of Mace.

It's like they just got caught in the act.
Guilt is written on every face.
As I make eye contact, with each of them,
not a one knows how to react,
or what to say.

I can only imagine what they've told them
about me—**THIS TIME**—contuinin' the trend.

Even though this is a crowded room,
amongst these so-called "family" 'n "friends."

I fight back these tears of pain.
As I'm standin', all alone,
once again . . .

THE TRUTH SHALL SET US FREE

All I've ever wanted t'be . . .
is ME.

And be the best me,
I could possibly be.

I've built myself up,
from the bottom up.
Now I'm callin' y'bluff . . .
Anyone that doesn't like it,
that's tough . . .

for all of us—it's been rough.

I would never have a need to lie.
If that's your "witty defense" . . .
well, that's a nice fuckin' try!

I'm tired of this victim cry.
I'm tired of always havin'
to ask myself: "Why?"

Why me?
Why him?
Why her?

Why was my seedhood
such a fuckin' blur?

Why did I force myself
to forget—so much?

The abuse . . .

the chaos . . .
the hunger . . .
'n such . . .

Why did I feel the need?

Why weren't they on the list
of the people whom leaves
needed to feed?

Why did they take a backseat
to alcohol, 'n gift-related
greed?

Why did they hit them, 'n make
them bleed?

Why was that pedophile
allowed in their home,
fully freed?

Why wasn't a leaf there,
in those horrific times
of need?

Most importantly, to me . . .
why did I allow any of y'all
to succeed!?

You really fucked me up
inside.

You're the reason I chose
all of this misplaced anger
to hide.

I had no one with whom I felt safe,
or remotely strong enough,
in which—to confide.

Why?
Why?
MOTHERFUCKIN' WHY!?

"He's got no reason t'be
upset."

"His upbringin' was not
a mess."

"He should jus' keep to himself,
like all of the rest."

"I can't wait to read what he thinks
caused all of his stress."

"There's nothin' for him to get
off of his chest."

AHHHHHHHHHHHHHHHHHH!

These are the words that've fueled
my poetic fire.

These are the lies that've antagonized
my utmost desire.

These are the downplayin',
self-centered,
"don't take anythin' he says serious"
types of bullshit statements that've helped me
get back up on my own two feet

'n hold my fuckin' head **HIGHER** . . .

knowin' that, one day,
everyone will know,
FULL WELL—who's really the g'damn liar.

And I pride myself on my integrity,
'n bein' a person that so many admire.

NO ONE can match my desire.

All I've ever wanted t'be . . .
is ME.

And be the best me,
I could possibly be.

I've built myself up,
from the bottom up.
Now I'm callin' y'bluff . . .
anyone that doesn't like it,
that's tough . . .

JUDGMENT DAY

Why do they feel
that their "holiness"
exempts them from
my retaliation?

They're the cause of
my anxiety . . .
my pain . . .
my stress . . .

my low tolerance . . .
my fuckin' humiliation!

Don't they realize that
they're livin' a shelf life,
with a date of expiration?

What if I were their
final judgement?
Remove the Good Lord
from **THIS** equation.

How would they fare,
with all of the
bullshit they bear,
in each fucked-up situation?

What if I were the one
that they had to answer to
when they finally reached
their ultimate destination?

How would they feel?

Better yet . . .
how would they deal?

With findin' out that I was,
the entire time,
their salvation.

What if I were given
that permission?
Would they be comfortable
with His decision?

They like to hide behind
their religious faith . . .
YET, THEY PICK 'n CHOOSE
THE RULES OF THEIR RELIGION!?

Thankfully,
I'm not that guy.
I want no part of
a spiritual collision.

But someday . . .
someday they're gonna
have to come to terms
with ALL of their religious
conditions, 'n traditions.

If they're goin' to
live a life of sin,
they'd better be prepared
to admit to their faults,
when they kneel down to
beg for forgiveness, for all
of their life's contradictions.

Only God . . .

POETIC SUICIDE

"Writin' the contents
of this book almost
killed me . . ."—rome

Seems like lately
I'm always fightin' back

these stress-filled tears.

Think, to yourself—for a moment.

How many times,
in your life,
have you forced yourself
to face ALL OF your
deepest, most darkest fears?

As I'd been wadin' my way
through (once-purposely buried) memories,
it finally caught up with me.
Relivin' all those troublesome years . . .

May 5, 2015
Boys' night out
at the Red Sox Game,
where I had so much
personal anguish
on my mind.

On that beautiful night,
inside of Fenway Park,
God, slowly, bestowed upon me
sign after sign.

As my body started to fail me,
I had this gut feelin',
that it was my time.

While I tried to gather my composure,
my thoughts switched gears,
'n you became the TOP thing
on my mind.

I struggled to catch my breath.
It was a feelin' that
I'd never wanted to
have to describe.

For the first time in my life,
I legitimately fear that
"I AM ABOUT TO DIE!"

Literally, leanin'—towards the sky.

But the fear wasn't for myself.
It was for our FAMILY.

It was for EVERYONE,
that I'd be forced
to leave—behind.

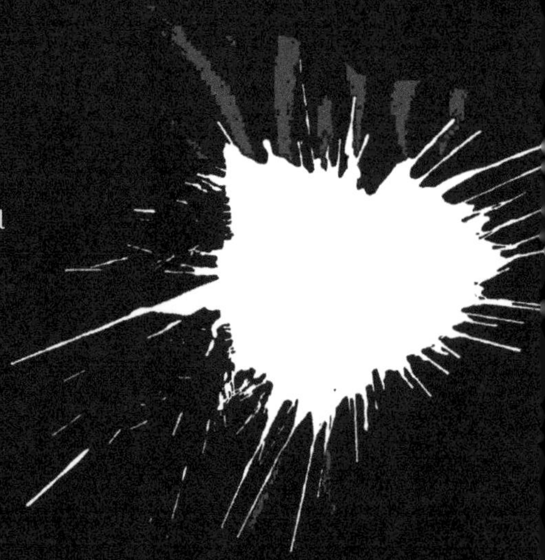

This wasn't like my occasional
thoughts—of suicide . . .
'cause, over those,
I've always had self-control.

Who'd have thought
that writin' about my past
would take this much
of a strenuous toll.

I'd dug the deepest
I've ever been able.
Into the most secured,
'n sometimes intimate,
areas of my soul.

As I'm sittin' in the stands
there's a tinglin' sensation,

down my left arm,
to my fingertips.

A sudden feelin' of pain,
in the back of my head.
My jaw is slowly tightenin'.
I've a quiver, in my lips.

Nausea floods my stomach.
Followed by a sudden dizziness.

I'm thinkin' . . . "I need to eat somethin'.
And I need t'do it—**QUICK**!"

But, still, I wait to tell my friend G-Dubb . . .
'til a third out—a swing, 'n a miss.

I finally stand up,
from my seat.

My knees are weak, 'n shakin'.
"I can't believe I'm goin' out—like this."

I force myself to climb the stairs.
I'm extremely short of breath.

Intentionally forcin' myself to cough,
while slowly pacin' the aisle.
Step, by wobbly step.

I pray to GOD:
"Please save me!
I'm not ready.
I'm literally scared to death!
Please, don't allow me to succumb
to my anxiety, 'n stress."

I couldn't' tell you what I'm lookin' like,
but I know I'm feelin'
like a complete 'n utter mess!

After standin' there for what seemed like an eternity . . .
WRONG LINE!
They're only servin' alcoholic beverages.

By now I'm in a panic.
While tryin' not to become frantic.
I run over to the concession stand . . .
"I need two hot dogs, 'n a drink."
She can tell that I'm on the brink—I think.
'Cause she hands me my food
straight over the glass . . .
I'm about t'go down—right on my ass.
I rush around the line,
'n toss the cashier my cash.

As I start shovin' the hot dog into my mouth,
my throat closes, with every failed attempt.
My body's not allowin' it to pass.
So, I quickly open up my Powerade,
'n chug it—down the hatch.

Now it's the "seventh-innin' stretch."
I've gotta tell my friends,
"I really need to leave."
I'm feelin' quite embarrassed,
'n I don't want them t'be peeved.

But I do so, knowin' (obviously)
what they could see.

I begin the walk back to the car.
Might I add, quite gingerly.

Once my head hits the headrest,
I pass out, from Boston to Dudley . . .

The next day I awoke,
'n made my way to work,
knowin' that my fiancé was
settin' up a visit—with my PCP.

Around 10 A.M. I receive a phone call.
She's talkin' quite frantically.

"YOU NEED TO GO TO THE ER,
RIGHT NOW—TO BE SEEN!
THEY THINK YOU HAD A HEART ATTACK!
YOU NEED TO TAKE THIS SERIOUSLY!"

The ambulance arrived, at my work . . .
a ride I'd hoped I'd never see.

LIFE UNSCRIPTED

Not everyone you trust is trustworthy.
Not every accepted friendship is a friend.
Not every request for help makes you vulnerable.
Not every poem written comes to a happy end.

I firmly believe that writin' poetry
is the art of exposin' feelings,
that only one's mind knows exist.

Sometimes I use it to speak candidly,
from the heart.

Other times the help of my anger,

TAPPED YET UNROOTED

I belligerently enlist.

I could count the family members
that I regularly associate with
on my left hand—which includes the thumb . . .
that I missed.

Okay,
I deliberately skipped.

But still includes the one I flipped,
after they were all tucked into a fist.

Four . . .

hours of sleep.
That's all I get.

I constantly weep . . .
feelin' so upset.

While I stay up late,
'n over-fret.

I'm over it.
My mind is set . . .

Everyone thinks they know
what's best for me.
But they don't care to
scratch the surface.

What they really want
is what's best for THEM.
They're not interested

in my life's purpose.

What if I told you that
I've been depressed for some many years?

That I hide all of my ill feelings,
behind confidence 'n reputation.

What if you found out
that my confidence is merely
a facade . . . for my peers?

That I've built it up knowin'
that I'm under constant re-evaluation?

. . . that writin' has become my salvation.

The cardiologist told me that stress
would be eminent to my death,
if I didn't find a way to release it.

Immediately, I had to decrease it.

So, now I'm on my rome shit

. . . my *I just wanna be known* shit
. . . my *don't wanna talk on the phone* shit
. . . my *just leave me alone* shit
. . . my *pour my feelings into a poem* shit.

This is MY life, in case you missed it.
This is my **LIFE UNSCRIPTED**.

SPARRIN' SESSION

My whole intent
behind writin' this isht,
was never to come off
as some bitter-ass bitch.

For real, though . . .

I really have no need for any
of the negativity, in which,
I'm forced to pop off
like that coward-esque snitch.

I will, though . . .

These are the thoughts
that cause my nervous twitch.
My heart to tighten up—those anxiety fits.

I'm so sick of my name bein' dragged
into "unnecessary" bullshit.

"I DEDICATE THIS THOUGHT
TO ANYONE OUT THERE
THAT CAN RELATE TO IT!"

To know that you're not alone,
when it comes to this shit.

I'm fightin' with you.
You 'n I, we coexist.

Together we can persevere
in our separateness.

I'll *hhhhock* enough force
for the both of us,
with every response that I spit.

They'll be so overpowered,
by our undeniable wit,
that they'll feel it for days.
EVERY LAST FUCKIN' HIT!
You see . . .
I entered this process
with a clear view—in sight.
I would write every g'damn word,
with both fists upright.

Fully prepared, for a lopsided fight.

Every lie they ever told . . .
well, that gave me the right
to defend myself, by any means necessary.
Even if it meant—defense out of SPITE.

With my back against the ropes,
I'd ball 'em up real tight,
'n throw haymakers of abusive words
in every possible direction (they'd take flight),
with all of my fuckin' might.

One by one
I'd knock them out . . .

all the way out . . .
OF MY LIFE.

I'm the undisputed champion.
Against all odds.
Against all strife.

I've been trainin' for this shit,
my entire life.

I fear not a single man.
Nor an ignorant, to the truth,
bitch of tree strife.

Now that my back's pressed
firmly against these ropes,
there's no place, for that knife.

Jus' sayin' . . .

Meet me toe-to-toe,
'n it's lights out—good night!

OMFG! MYOB TEXT

J'd up—from head to toe.
White boy—with a poetic flow.

He says the shit—they're scared to think.
Pushin' feelings—to the brink.

His thoughts are filled—of starved ink.
Now it's a feedin' frenzy—of carved fink.

When you're caught up
in the struggle,
there's no such thing—as success . . .

It's more like:
"What the fuck-cess!?"
'n

“What the fuck’s sex?”
‘n
“What the fuck’s next?”

Ahhhhhhhhh!

Sometimes life becomes
far too difficult—to juggle . . .
I guess.

Like wakin’ up—to a fucked-up text.

beeping
beeping

I text back: “Hey, what’s good?”

They say that she’s
contracted STDs,
from CODs . . .

‘n here I am—at home,
in my BR—SMH!

[sarcasm]

“Just gr8!”

[end sarcasm]

That’s a little bit TMI
for this guy.
I’m like FYI,
IDC how she
intimately relates.

Furthermore, IDGAF
about the narcotics
that she accumulates.

WTF is wrong with her leaf?
Whom she—to a g'damn T—
perfectly emulates. RT . . .

They'll be SOL
if they think those drugs
are gonna sit around—'n wait.

You don't just tempt
the hands of fate.

Oh wait . . .
BRB
GGP
1SEC

OK
I'm back . . .
Where was I?

OIC . . .

Yeah, we were talkin' 'bout
a RL family problem,
before I went OT.

My B!

From my POV,
I just get so upset
havin' to hear about
this type of mess.

FWIW—I hate seein' either of them
in such agonizin' distress.

But IMO,
she should've done
a little more parentin',
'n a LOT less "LYLAS."

But WTH do I know?

THAT TIME OF THE MONTH

I know that we're not supposed to hate.
But, right now, hatred floods my heart.

Born with a gapin' hole within it . . .
this pool's been tainted—from the start.

Its capabilities have been
accurately measured.
The ratings are flyin'—off the chart.

For their sake,
I hope shit floats.

'Cause they've all boarded
a sinkin' ark.

Two by two their animalistic
lies have boarded.

But fairly soon,
they'll each be torn apart.

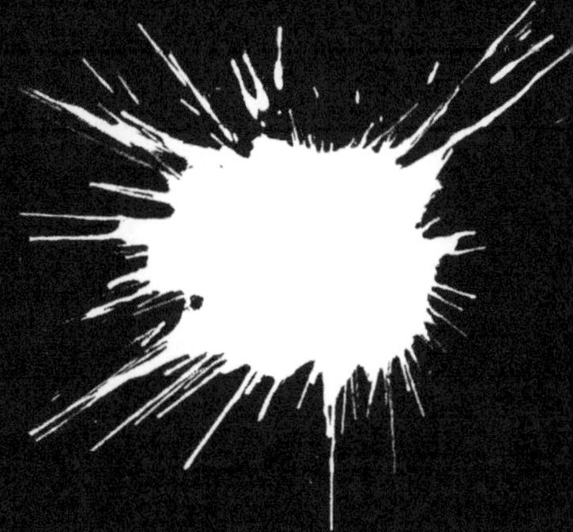

TAPPED YET UNROOTED

Those that say
"blood is thicker than water"
are 'bout to witness the poetic word slaughter,
by a precisely calculative
great white "roman" shark.

"I've seen this shit before.
Quick, someone sound the alarm!
The type of damage that rome
quick wittedly administers
has been known to cause
insurmountable harm."

But, for them—it's already too late.
I've opened up the flood gate.

Every single lie they've ever told about me,
will be drown—like I submerged the entire farm.

Then, once they're rendered lifeless,
'n 'bout to rise to the top . . .

I'ma sink my teeth right through each fib,
'n savor them—'til that very last drop.

I'm makin' sure that EVERY fuckin' untruth
they've ever happily told
has (PERMANENTLY) been stopped!

Shit, I'm so fuckin' tired,
of all their bloody drama,
that I'ma end this poem—with a comma,
and save the "periods"
for those lip-leakin' li'l bitches
that chummed my waters
through their feministic britches . . .

Tread lightly . . .
you untruthful,
less-than-useful,
blood-spillin',
tampon-fillin',
snitches . . .

whose lies, like a fish outta water,
have flopped,

AB •WAY •LOW •BLOW

I'm not sayin' what I hate.
But, I'm not hatin' what I say . . .

I'm not placin' any bids.
'Cause what I'm sayin' is not forbidden . . .

I'm not happy to have been dissed.
But I'm not unhappy about the distance . . .

I'm not quite sure about what you did.
But it's quite clear as to what you didn't . . .

I'm not sayin' that you're missed.
But I'm not braggin' 'bout what you're missin' . . .

I'm not talkin' 'bout your kids.
But I'm not talkin' like I'm kiddin' . . .

I'm not sayin' you've been rid.
I guess what I'm sayin' is . . .

Good riddance!

IF I'M BEIN' HONEST

My tree loves to play
all sorts of games.
We're atypical in this fashion.

You might be surprised
by the blurred lines
that we'll all climb
above 'n across,
in order to make
the ridiculous happen.

Now, I'm nowhere close
to bein' proud
of any of our actions.

The games I'm referrin' to
don't involve boards.
Seeds are used as pawns.
There's no laughter,
nor the involvement of buzzers
when we're slappin'.

In case you're still clueless
as to what's 'bout to happen:

I'm talkin' 'bout the petty games.
Those childish games.
The games in which
there's no winner,
'n everyone loses.
The ones that lead to
telephone confrontations
'n scrappin'.

Push comes to shove.
Enough is enough.

When I start to lose self-control,
my gums also start flappin'.

I subconsciously bite my lip.
Tilt my brows.
Clench my fist.
Then I black out,
'n don't remember isht.

There's only so much I can take,
before I wind up snappin'.

Now we're layin' down the smack, 'n
I'm a verbal assassin.

'Cause when I finish puttin'
their bullshit to rest,
I get everythin' off
my fuckin' chest,
'n rest assured that
my opponents' feelings
are in a casket—dirt nappin'.

But this hibernation
only lasts for so long.

It never matters
who's right,
or wrong.

You see,
instead of playin'
hide 'n go seek,

we play forgive
'n pretend that shit
didn't happen.

Which is why,
like a fool,
ONE keeps on actin'.

Their favorite seed
can do no wrong.

Lemme just throw
that last (important)
fact in.

HOLD THE DESSERT

I'm fresh off of
bein' slandered
by this seed.

Hell,
the entire tree knew
before I ever did.

Of this family member's
unprovoked remarks
about my supposed
"sexual preference" that
to me they've recently un-hid.

Which caused me to pop off,
at the mouth,
'n lose my fuckin' lid!

Now, here I am
celebratin' the holidays,
at another family seed's crib.

And a LEAF thinks it'd be funny
to crack a gay joke
at my expense,
in front of our tree
(includin' the in-laws),
'n all of our kids.

The looks on everyone's faces,
had me wishin' I could've
crawled under the table,
in the fetal position—'n hid.

The moment they said:
"If you could, you know
you would totally go gay,
for an athlete from the
game that you love t'play!"

Yep . . . once again,
ANOTHER member
of my tree
felt the need to
try 'n clown me,
durin' dinner,
on that particular day.

On CHRISTMAS EVE . . .
in front of EVERYONE . . .

What would YOU do?
How would YOU react?
What would YOU say?

My initial reaction
was to immediately
put their ass at bay.

Yeah, FUCK IT!
You only live once . . .
what the hey.

And in one sentence,
I subconsciously went
to town on 'em!

"This comin' from the person,
that if their favorite QB walked in,
they'd drop to their knees
'n go right down on 'em!"

laughter

awkward pause

Now, if you can,
just imagine the
angry frown on 'em.

Guess they weren't
expectin' me to
turn it around on 'em.

And just like that,
for the second
consecutive time,
I've allowed myself
to stoop to this
immature level.

In disbelief,
I couldn't even begin
to think—to revel.

Out of respect,
I'm not usually
the one to
lash out—or bicker.

This quick-witted exchange
couldn't have happened
any quicker.

For the record:
I fully own up to
my involvement.

But here's the
"laugh out loud"
kicker . . .

THEY expected an apology . . .
from ME!?

My stomach couldn't
possibly feel
any sicker.

After bein' coerced
to defend my integrity,
through a half-hearted
snicker.

This sucks!

BREAKIN' IT DOWN

"Curse-word caring"
is a concept I've created,
to give my family
an assessment of the value
of my swear.

It's still a prototype, though.
Buyer beware!

Don't you just hate it
when someone disrespects you
either by mouth,
or a resentful glare?

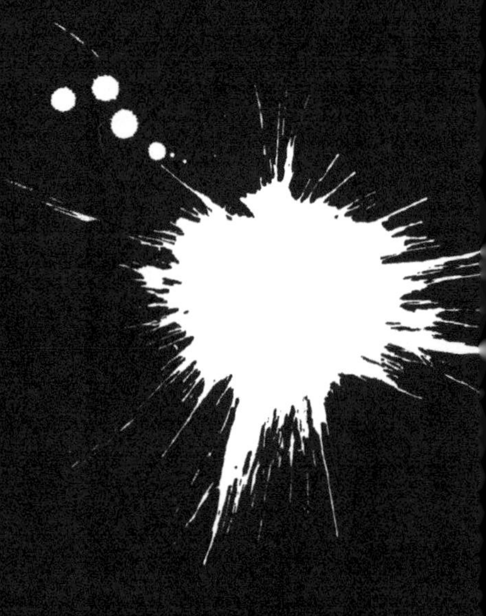

Pay close attention
to what I do here.

Usually this is the moment where
I give away all of my fucks.
They really compliment
a nasty stare.

But, I've already handed out
all of my fucks today.
I've not a single fuck left
to share.

When I do give a fuck,
that fuck which I gave,
was for the sole purpose of showin'
someone how much I care.

So . . .

if I did not offer them a fuck today,
it's because not a fuck to them
did I wanna give.

I repeat . . .
when I don't give a fuck,
not a fuck do I care enough
to give.

It's all quite relative,
in the problem-filled life
that I live.

Speakin' of relatives . . .
sometimes, when I run out
of fucks to give,
I'll instead hand out two shits.

Now, shits . . .
shits are a double-edged sword.
I've learned (when used properly)
they tend to hit the right chord.

We all know that
no one likes t'be given shit.
But, when you don't give a shit,
the same people get pissed
about bein' ignored.

(Which also applies to fucks.)

Now, remember,
two shits
are the equivalent
of a single fuck.

So, it's only appropriate
that two shits
is what I refuse to give
to these pricks.

'Cause when someone isn't
worth two shits,
not a single shit
do they receive.

You see . . .
I'm not really known t'be
one to deceive.
But every once in a while,
when they piss me off,
I'll be sly 'n withhold,
from them, a damn.

It's worth a lot less
than two shits,
but I can usually sneak it by
the naive members
of my fam.

Which, in most cases
regardin' the fam,
I generally don't
give a damn.

And . . .
since one fuck
is the equivalent
of two shits,
because a single shit
fails by marginal
comparison,

be sure not to ever get
a fuck mixed up
with a damn,
'cause mixin' up that shit
can get extremely fuckin'
embarrassin'.

INITIALIZED

Sticks 'n stones may break my bones,
but sometimes this name
really fucks me up—inside.

You can say most anythin',
but don't you ever antagonize
my PRIDE!

Dangerous is thinkin'
that I won't bite
a hand that feeds me.

I've been force-fed
so much bullshit lately,
that my stomach's been feelin' queasy.

The mere thought
of digestin' anymore shit
has my innards restin' uneasy.

I've tried, time 'n time again, to let it go.
I know, without a doubt,
that this feud is beneath me.

I'm not takin' anythin'

out of this relationship.
You can keep my half—discretely.

It's time I walk away—for good.
For your sake,
you'd better not prod, nor tease me.

It's already taken everythin' I have
to let you off—**THIS** g'damn easy.

I'ma walk away now.
You can go.
Please, just leave me.

This time I've turnt my back—for good.
They'd better hope that they never need me.

I need a serious reprieve . . .
from the family crest—that impedes me.
A legal separation would (more than) please me.

And if that separation led to a divorce . . .
well, then, that might also appease me.

What's in a name?
Lyin',
backstabbin',
manipulatin',
non-loyal—all around fuckin' sleazy.

A substantial break is in order,
from my government name, 'cause . . .
she's become so (permanently) attached.

Everywhere I go, she precedes me.
Like an online stalker—I've met my match.

Upon our "initial" meetin', an automobile doctor
determined I was quite the fighter—to catch.
Then J. had Missus E. slip two E's
in harmony, so "hEr monEy"
would be placed on a junior—facts.

Yes, I was born J.E.E., Jr.—
for those of you still tryin' to figure out
the relativity in which I was "initially" hatched.

If I'd have known then,
that adoption was an option,
then the surname I dated all these years
wouldn't have a need t'be legally detached.

I've already removed her from my basketball jersey.
I no longer carry her burden—on my back.

I've been goin' with "rome" for a while now.
Everyone knows that name t'be a class act.
Not t'be confused with the crazy
that the other one can attract.

Even though I treat her like a vindictive ex,
for better, or for worse—I'm trapped.
'Til death do us part—it's a wrap.

Like a straitjacket, to my last name—I'm strapped.

"rome,
your fuckin' tree! It's unrooted, yet tapped."

Tapped, yet unrooted? No CRAP!
Tell me somethin' I didn't know . . .

NOTE TO SELF

Dear rome,

Sometimes, when love is blind,
the only happiness you'll find
lies within the seeds left behind
durin' a forcefully assigned bind . . .
Blacked out, then lost your g'damn mind,
'n said so many words that were unkind
(slingin' names, 'n curse words, in a seamless line)
because on that particular date in time,
that's the way you were designed.

You'd never been one to act refined.
Which is really the main reason why,
I can't believe you went 'n signed,
along that institutionalized dotted line,
knowin' that one day could potentially find,
your beautiful seeds similarly aligned
in a situation like mine . . .
yours . . .
OURS . . .

You'd convinced me that you were happy.
But to **YOURSELF**, you lied.

That night we were served one last meal.
Since the judgment had already been applied.
Our sentence was predetermined, when rendered.
No matter how hard we repeatedly tried,
any shot at returnin' to our seeds,
several times, was adamantly denied.

You see,

while we're the type that's content
with a small, brownish/green patch,
"as long as I can call it MINE."

Others seem to believe that
"the grass is always greener,
on the other side."

The jurors had already found themselves
a greener pasture, 'n our small patch
of grass—had completely died.

Addin' to the landscape of a blindside,
we'd never been away from our seeds
for a sentence of this length of time.
So, on that day, part of us also died—
with a feelin' of incarceration bein' applied.

That entire car ride, we shook 'n cried.
The pain, we felt, would not subside.
Livin' without our seeds—weighed heavily
on our newly panic-stricken mind.
Then came (back) those thoughts—of suicide,
that could've resulted in our last car ride.

As we handed Jesus the wheel despite
closin' both of our eyes—real tight,
'n pullin' with both hands to the right.
Had we lost our willingness to fight,
'n tried to end it all—that night?

We'd smashed our cellular device
off the dash.
Everythin' spiraled out of control
within a flash.

TAPPED YET UNROOTED

It's a wonder we didn't up 'n crash.
We can be such a fuckin' SELFISH ASS!
What would those seeds do, without their dad?
We'd be lucky with a spin out in greener grass.

Oh, that beautiful grass . . .
a second chance, at life.
A half-full glass.
A "greener beginning" . . .
some much-needed time to learn—
from the contrast.

Another failed suicide attempt?
A spur-of-the-moment decision?
No questions asked.

Dammit, rome!
Listen up . . .
I've saved some important advice
for last:

It's time to let go—of the past!

We need to learn to pump the breaks,
on those suicidal thoughts,
'n remove our foot—from the gas.

Let's take our time, in the future.
It's important that we stop ourselves
from actin' so damn crass.

And, for the love of God,
don't be in such a rush to plant new grass.

Find a nice girl . . .
settle down,

‘n make HER our last.

The next six years with our seeds
are gonna fly by—so fast.
I PROMISE!

P.S. We’re really gonna enjoy
that anger management class . . . lol

Sincerely,
rome

COMPASSIONATE

“Tell me who needs t’be handled,
and it’s done!”
—DMC

. . . and they’re all wonderin’ why,
whenever DMC is in a Jam,
like Master Jay—I Rev. up, ‘n Run!?

“C’mon, son . . .”

There’s so much that she’s, already,
been forced to overcome.

The very least I can do—is help HER out some.
If ever someone deserved it—she’d be the one.

SHE’S the matriarch—of our tree!
The glue—that binds everyone together.

It’s because of her undyin’ selflessness,

that countless storms I've been able to weather.

She's the one that believes she can save the world.
By world, I mean every single family grievance.

She's the one that (behind her back) they refer to
as "nothin' but a lying bitch!"
Yet, she's the first one to reach out, 'n call them . . .
to congratulate them—on any/all of their achievements.

Wanna talk about stress!?

She's the ONLY one that forgives, 'n forgets.
She's the ONLY one that harbors no ill feelings—or regrets.
She's also the ONLY one that over-obsessively frets,
whenever family members complain—of their financial debts.

Always searchin' for ways to help others.
Even when she's havin' issues—helpin' herself.
We've always been a tree "of meager beginnings"
in regards to personal possessions 'n wealth.

Not to mention the fact that (currently)
she's really not in the best of health.

But, call her when you're in need,
'n she forgets all about the hand she's been dealt.

It doesn't matter how (at that time)
she may, or may not—have felt.

With all that said,
she certainly doesn't deserve any
of the treatment that she's been receivin'.

This shit's got me shakin' my head.

If I were her, I'd have already fled.
They treat her like their relationship's dead.

That is . . .
until her services/help—they're needin'.
Or her ears, when rumor mill bullshit—they're feedin'.

. . . only call her for a ride to the store
. . . only call her for a key when you're outside of a locked door
. . . only call her to tell her that So 'n so died, 'n so many more
. . . only call her to complain about "dizzy spells" galore
. . . only call her when times get tough.
Again . . . when the hell is enough—ENOUGH!?

YES, she's got an extremely kind heart.
But they're constantly snatchin' it—'n trashin' it.

Which led us here . . .
I don't care . . .
I'm askin' it.

What the hell happened to bein'
COMPASSIONATE?

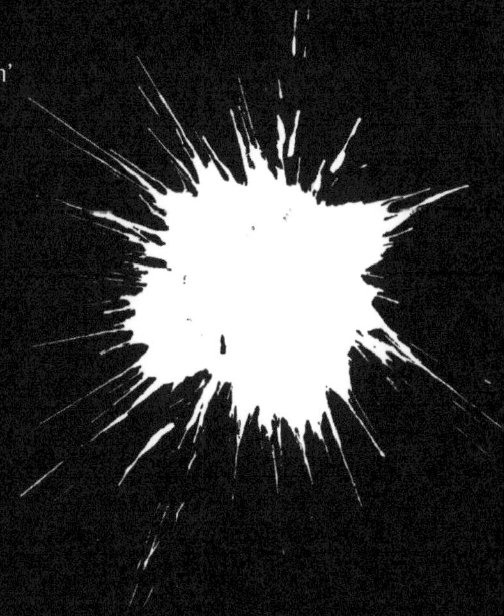

JEALOUS MUCH

You may as well
be a relative.
You're as shady
as the rest.

How much more effort
can a fella give!?

TAPPED YET UNROOTED

When all of your actions,
I detest.

You're leakin' like
a hella sieve.

Out of every pore,
you just don't rest . . .

I can't understand the anger.
I can't understand the angst.
I can't understand the envy
that appears t'be your face.

I don't understand the resentment.
I'm a family man, devout.

Usually pink elephants are irrelevant.
If I might say so myself.

But it's gotten so bad,
that I had to ban you.

You're no longer welcome,
in or around
our house.

Yet, you're still present
at all of our functions.

You spend so much
of your time,
lingerin' about.

Hell . . .
I've even noticed you,

straight up,
grillin' me . . .

whenever we cookout.

Hey, Jealousy . . .

you're a bitter bitch.
One which I can live—
WITHOUT!

You may as well be a relative.

CLEAR THE AIR

Their rumors will never define me.
Most of the shit they say—it's absurd.

I walk the walk.
I talk the talk.

I'll disprove every negative lie—about me—
that you've ever heard.

I'm a walkin' blueprint.
Unduplicated.
One of a kind.

He broke the mold,
when He gave me my soul.

Not another, like me,
will you ever find.

I poured my heart
into that fucker.

I practically grew them,
as if they were mine.

We did the best that we could
as seeds, waterin' a seed.
Together . . .
them 'n I.

Slowly they started to change.
I can't really pinpoint
an accurate time.

To my face
everythin' was great.
We got along—just fine.

It started out
with the news—of one lie.

That one lie
turned into lies.

Those lies turned into rumors.
Those rumors—I fuckin' despise.

One day they're tellin' people I'm gay:
"He's been single for too long.
I think he's into guys."

The next day I'm a man-whore.
"He's bangin' every female
who openly complies."

They've even spread a rumor
to our immediate family
regardin' my "dick size."
(I can't make this shit up.)

What kind of a relative
gets off on spreadin' such lies,
about a guy's "wanderin' eye"?

Let that sink in.

But not too deep.

I'd hate to see the validity
of this rumor compromised.

I mean, I've heard of penis envy.

But . . .
to hate, because I'm circumcised?
To hate, because I'm one of the guys?
To hate, because I'm datin' females,
while you sat at home 'n fantasized?

Nothin' better for you t'do
than to, falsely, narrate my life.

I hope you enjoyed it—while it lasted.
You won't get that opportunity twice.

I no longer entertain these lies.
I no longer have to say you're here, too.

Shit,
you can take back your fork-tongue'd knife.

I've got enough holes
in my back—to suffice.

SEE WHAT YOU MADE ME DO

Why does HE always feel
the need to "knock down" me?

Why does SHE always feel
the need to "talk 'round" me?

Why does "So 'n so" always feel
the need to "mock 'n clown" me?

Why does my mind always
feel the need to "stalk 'n hound" me?

Jottin' down thoughts,
while feelin' depressed.

Chasin' down acceptance,
in the form of success.

Contemplatin' suicide—life after death.
It's hard to explain—without goin' in depth.

Wonderin', when all is said 'n done,
with this craziness,
what (exactly) will I have left . . .

"behind"
. . . by way of my legacy?

I often think deeply,

without ill intent.

The questions I ask myself,
would leave most *verklempt.*

Since I read like an open book,
there's no chapter exempt.

Let's skip towards the middle . . .
a well-thought-out attempt.

If I died tomorrow,
what should you have said?

Could you let me go,
without harborin' regrets?

Was the time that we shared,
full of memorable events?

Did we build the relationship,
that you felt was meant?

Did I do enough—in my lifetime,
to become Heaven-sent?

Or . . .

if I didn't leave a note . . .
would they consider foul play?

If I did leave a note . . .
would I have found the right words—to say?

'N if I did—would it really matter?
Could life, beyond livin'—make me even sadder?

I certainly don't wanna see Hell,
nor a fireman's ladder.
So, burnin' myself—that's not an option.

I'm not tryin' to drown, either.
So, the bathtub nor water—I'm tryin' neither.
We can place that idea—up for adoption.

Hangin' myself—with a homemade noose?
What if I just snapped my neck,
'n lost the use—of my limbs . . .
then I'd be nothin' more than
a bed-ridden recluse,
who's STILL of no use—to his kids.

How could I ever look them
in their eyes again—if I did?

Instead I grabbed the bottle—popped the lid.
One by one, down my throat—they slid.

waited

Then, frantically, changed my mind.
On but only several pills—had I dined.
Still frantically (possibly unnecessarily),
down my throat—I insert my finger.
Not for very long, does it deeply linger.
Until I, anxiously, threw my innards up.
And this desperate attempt—ends rather abrupt.

A secret I've (forever) hid.
About my sporadic plan to rid—myself . . .
of this downward, flailin' skid.

Sometimes I'm so scared—of death . . .

that I make up all of these excuses
. . . to continue to live.

Other times I make a half-hearted attempt,
cry myself to sleep—on a cold floor's grid—
and wake up utterly embarrassed,
that I'd lost the will—like I did
. . . when I did,
. . . how I did.

I just didn't want to continue to live.
. . . with these thoughts inside my head,
. . . with all of the cruel words, that they've said,
. . . or without my beautiful kids.

SMH
I'm sorry.

Now you know why,
for so long this secret . . .
I'd hid.

YA-YA YEARNIN'

With a smile on my face,
we talk on for hours.

From the afternoon,
into the night.

Chattin' with him
provides intellectual stimulation,
while deliverin' some top-notch,
quality

insight.

He's always lookin'
for the positive light.

Which shines down,
upon our family tree.

From the progression
of our ancestors,
to those that fought,
for our country—in the military.

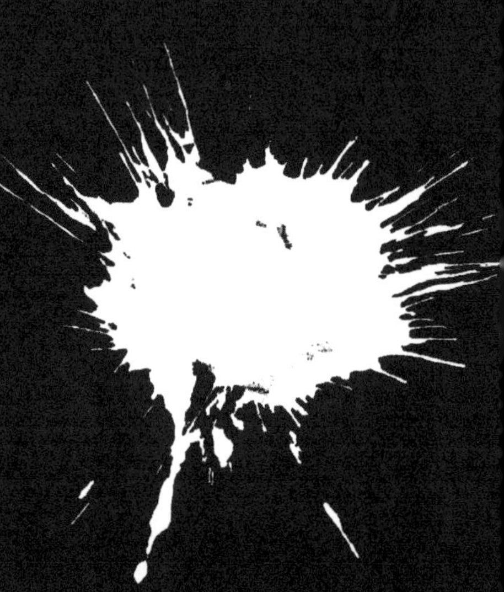

But he,
like me,
is also a seed.
He's no stranger—to adversity.

Although she made sure
that he always had . . .
he grew up without.
She's proven t'be all
that he'd need.

M'dude's one extremely
resilient Swede.

With a mindset that
often challenges my
intellectual need . . .

Here's one tiny snippet,
of the thought provokin' web,
that we, daily, weave . . .

He said:

"rome, let me ask you a question.
When you ask someone
how they're doin' . . .
do you really want a response?
Because when I say it,
I don't want a conversation.
I'm just tryin' t'be polite."

again, smilin'
I let that sink in.

Allow it to marinate—from within.

Y'know . . .
I think,
in a roundabout way,
he might be right.

We live in a world of
passive aggression.

Where greetin' someone
is nice—'n polite.

But we'd much rather do it
IN PASSIN'.

And continue on our way.
Keepin' our agenda—in sight.

ESPECIALLY if it's someone,
in the tree,
that we may not particularly like.

Jus' sayin' . . .

I'm not tryin' to add fuel
to the fight.

UNTIL WE MEET AGAIN/HERE TOO

I've reached a point,
in my thoughts,
where you were intricate
towards the plot.

But before I get into that,
I, first, want to speak (openly)
from my heart.

I've got so much I'd like
to say to you.

Gosh, where do I start?

I LOVE YOU, MY FRIEND!
That love will never depart.

One of my fondest memories of you
took place on the high school track.
Where you turned distance runnin' into your art.

You ran faster than a Wolfgang.
A 1600-meter Mozart.
I'll never forget that race, that day.
You were confident—from the start.

I can still picture you "Superman"
divin' (head first) over the FINISH line.
Then you looked at me, 'n smiled.

Thinkin' back, right now, it breaks my heart.

tears

I never would have imagined
that when LIFE ran its course,
we'd have grown so far apart . . .

{{{Rest in peace}}}
1977—2013

My li'l buddy.
My red-headed counterpart.

Opie,
Words couldn't possibly express my heartache,
when I first stepped foot, off of that plane . . .

to a text message readin'
"I'm so sorry for your loss"
wrapped around your name.

"This can't be happenin'!
It can't be true!" to my fiancée
I emphatically exclaimed.

In that moment,
I felt like such a horrible person,
for not knowin' that you were even sick.

I mean, I'd run into you sporadically,
but those interactions were always quick.

A "Hey! How are you doin'?"
then, just like that, we'd split.

I wish that—right then,
I had told you
how much you were truly missed.

Your smile.
Your funny laugh.
Your sense of humor.

All of which—I miss.

Gone, but not forgotten . . .
Your nickname's the only other one in this book.
Stayin' true to my word—just as I had promised.

You coined the phrase in this next thought.
But the name had t'be dismissed.

You 'n I'd go back 'n forth—
crackin' these jokes,
'n "I'm" would get so pissed.

Although no one will be mentioned,
I'll make sure our readers get the gist.

Let's try to gather a heavenly laugh
(the way we used to, with a personal twist).

My forever memory with you
goes a li'l somethin' like this:

For Opie,

I think that everyone has that ONE person
that wants t'be a part—of everythin' they do.

As if they become stuck to your hip,

like paper holds closely to glue.

Just Adam, “I’m,” ‘n myself.
We’re sittin’ outside, in the dark
on the front stoop.
As the cars drive by the house,
delegatin’ them (to each other)
is what Opie, ‘n I, liked t’do.

“You get that beat-up, old, pickup truck.
And I’ll take the brand-new Lexus coup!”

“Nah . . . you get that, two-toned, rusty Corolla.
And I’ll take the custom Honda,
with the chrome rims ‘n giant swoop!”

We’d been doin’ this for hours,
before a yell (from across the street)
came through.

“rome? Opie? Is that you?”

Then a soft voice, beside us, chimed in . . .

*"**Hey, hey! Say I’m here, too!**"*

This was the start of a trend,
between me ‘n my seedhood friend,
‘n some of the hilarity that ensued.

Some (overly embellished) jokes
at the expense of “I’m”?

Yeah, fuck it!
One last time—for old times’ sake . . .
here’s a few:

What's that you say?
rome went to the zoo?
Why wasn't I invited, to tag along,
on this trip with you?
I'd like to see a monkey, a zebra,
a "fuzzy li'l bunny," or a lazy emu.
Maybe I could have taken a photo,
while standin' with a baby kangaroo.
Then when people see that pic,
they could "say I'm here, too!"

Hold up . . . you're playin' basketball!?
Let's play a game of two-on-two!
Please, let me be the one
to throw that alley-oop
above the hoop—to you.
Sure, it'll look like a shot . . .
with an ugly follow through.
But after you dunk it home,
at least they'll "say I'm here, too!"

If you're goin' number one,
then I wanna go doo-doo.
Please, please, let me come
to the facilities with you.
You're gonna pee.
I'm gonna poo.
Then after I finish—droppin' a smelly clue,
if I'm really lucky,
the attendant might "say I'm here, too!"

You're gettin' ready to fight?
Please, please, *paa-leease* . . .
for the love of God,
let me stand **BEHIND** you.
Then after you knock 'em out,

I'll jump around—like a fool.
Air kickin' 'n screamin' **hyyy—ahh!**
like I know black belt kung fu.
So then when he comes back to,
he'll be a li'l bit groggy-headed,
but he can still "say I'm here, too!"

Damn, you're six-foot-three?
I'm like five feet, give or take a few.
Man, even in height—I look up to you.
Maybe if I climb up on your shoulders,
someone will notice ME—from that view.
Then maybe . . .
just maybe . . .
they'll "say I'm here, too!"

Huh?
Wait . . . wait . . . wait . . .

You heard I was tellin' everyone
outlandish lies, about you?
gulps
I guess an explanation is long overdue.

Well, I didn't think you'd find out.
See, THERE!
Right there.
I finally told the truth!
NOW can you mention **MY** name in this book?

"Hey, hey! Say I'm here, too!"

I promise you, rome.
Cross my heart, 'n hope t'be more like you.
You've got my absolute word,
that I will **NOT** threaten to sue.

That's just somethin' that someone
with a guilty conscience would try t'do.

And, with that last roast, I'm through.
Never again, will I speak about "I'm."

Yet,
if you were still here,
there's no doubt in my mind,
that you'd have a joke for "I'm,"
or quite a few.

They just don't hit the same, without you.
God, are you missed m'dude.

I love you, Ope.
Until we joke again, my friend:
"Hey, hey! Say I'm here, too!"

QUESTIONS 'N ANSWERS

How do you explain
to your seeds
that some of their
relatives flat-out suck?

When they're too young
to hear the bitter truth.

But when it comes to
receivin' an explanation,
they've proven that they're
old enough.

How do I explain to them
that—because of me,
TO YOU—they no longer exist?

Or why you didn't call them,
on their birthday,
nor the subsequent parties,
that you've missed?

What is the proper response—to a seed
that asks why you're always
so mean—to their father?

I don't know of a polite way to tell them
that you're just insensitive assholes.
So, for that, among many other reasons,
with you I no longer bother.

How do I teach them
to trust in one another,
because there's value in a lovin' tree?
In other words . . .
how do I teach them
to believe what I **USED TO** believe,
when they've witnessed the exact opposite
in relationships between some of you 'n me?

The answer to all of these questions is . . .
I don't.
I can't.
I won't.
I shan't.

You see, unlike you,
my seeds will never—ever—
hear me slander a relative's name.

Yes, I will always speak
on behalf of the truth.

But, never will I stoop
so low as to rally up a group
to kick off a smear campaign—of ANYONE'S name.

But as for y'all—I'll forever be ashamed.
Victimizin' seeds of all ages
to those antisocial games that y'all like to play.
Then you get pissed off at the ones
that chose not to follow the herd,
'n as you deem—defiantly go astray . . .

Thanks to you,
my outlook on family life
has, for the better,
been permanently changed.

Now my seeds
won't have to grow up,
like I did . . .

'cause they'll be estranged,
from the childish games.

NOT IT

If there's one thing that I take pride in,
it's the way that I'm perceived.

To become a better person,
is a daily goal—that I strive to achieve.
Sometimes their antics are so unthinkable,

it's hard for even myself—to believe.

My cellular's been blowin' up.
Several message notifications I've received.

It looks like (once again)
I'm gonna need t'be reprieved.

Someone's changed their network name,
'n others have identified it as me!?

This is just what I need . . .
more unsolicited controversy.

There's about a ninety-percent accuracy.
At first glance, they match—identically.
But the profile picture attached . . .
NOPE!
What a shock.
That's not ME!

It's a case of mistaken identity.

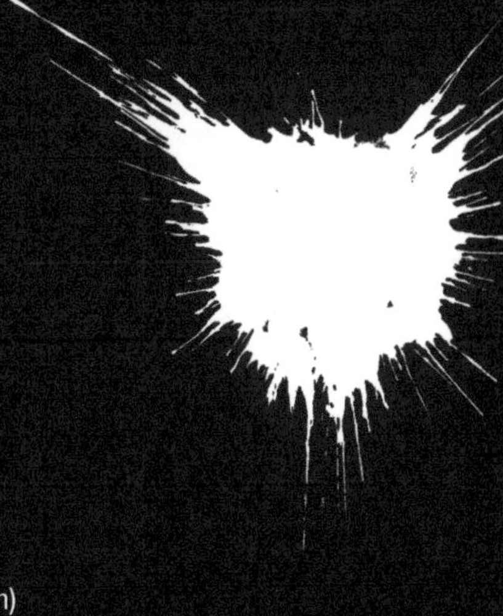

It's not at all cute to have to see
"likes" 'n comments by some
g'damn rome wannabe.

Underneath provocative pictures,
of a ("scantily clad") young teen.

Now I'm caught—in between
the way it is, 'n the way that it seems
towards a female—that never (in person)
have they seen.

The fact that they're even mutual friend

I find completely obscene!

Now, once again, it's up to me—to intervene.
As I'm explainin' to their significant other
how it's not at all what it seems.

What the fuck is wrong with YOU!?

On social media actin' a fool.
Settin' me up—for more ridicule.
To you this may seem minuscule.
But to my fire, you keep addin' fuel.
What part of you thought that
this would be any kind of cool?

Seriously, though.
This nonsense has reached its plateau.
I can no longer partake in this shit show.
As a person, I need some positive light
in order to help myself grow.

I've got seeds—that I need to show,
that there's no shame in lettin' go.

WRITIN' FIRE

A cloud of smoke
is all that remains
of my dirty laundry—bein' aired.

If you're readin' this,
then that might mean
I've finally reached someone—that cared.

This verbal onslaught
had been smolderin'
for quite some many years.

With my internal flame
continuously fueled
by the overflow of external tears.

Allow me to make one thing
abundantly clear:

Once my stylus pen
feels any signs of friction,
the slightest spark of emotion
ignites my disregard for fear.

I'm currently as fearless
as one might appear.
Despite these circumstances,
which I've attempted to forbear.

Which is how we've arrived,
in the current position
that we're in—right here.

Some refer to my poetic style
as "writin' fire."

. . . 'Cause my thoughts 'n beliefs
are concurrently gettin' torched.

I recently learned my lesson—the hard way
on how to deal
with writer's remorse.

There were no limits

to the depths that I'd stoop.
There wasn't a topic
which I wouldn't use—as a last resort.

The one time I allowed myself
to play too closely to my thoughts,
my heart gets slightly scorched.

I'd been toyin' with my own emotions,
while blazin' up witty retorts . . .
in response to false allegations,
'n numerous (slanderous) reports.

It took me weeks to fully recover,
from that coronary attack.
I've never felt that out of sorts.

For years, I'd been told
by tree members
that I should just keep
my thoughts to myself.

It's no secret that,
for the past umpteen months,
I've been verbally burnin'
this chaotic life that I've been dealt.

Now everybody's "shocked" 'n "concerned"
that doin' as they'd requested
has been detrimental—to my health.

They know my thoughts are money.

I know that karma has a funny way,
of redistributin' the wealth . . .

now, all of a sudden,
they've become fully understandin'
towards the way that I have felt.

It seems THEIR thoughts are sinkin' in,
as to what they might
have to soon endure—themselves.

"rome's been writin' fire!
It's every relative for him/herself . . ."

Got a guilty conscience?
I've got some advice, that just might help:

Start actin' like decent human beings!

Then I'll fold back up YOUR laundry,
'n place it on a clean-slate shelf.

Hell, I'll even go back
to keepin' my thoughts—about life
to MYSELF.

THE SETUP

Straight edge 'n sober.
That's the explanation,
for my entire life . . .

I have no fallback excuses
for any of the shit—that I write.

(As a result of seedhood plight . . .
the only time I black the fuck out

is when I get into a physical altercation
that leads to a fisticuff fight.

. . . 'n I remember every fuckin' thing
from that night!)

I know—for an absolute fact
that the shit they've said about me
just ain't frickin' right.

But I'ma forever defend myself . . .
you can bet your ass.
You're g'damn right!

They believe that I've got ice water,
steady flowin',
throughout my veins.

" . . .'n rome's got thirsty bitches
bringin' they 'cups'—to the tap,
waitin' for a break
in his main"

. . . is the type of fucked-up
bullshit they keep on sayin'.

Yet, I'm not the type t'be
relationship slippin' . . .

They must be insane—straight-up trippin'.
They need to stay in their lane—while lip-whippin'.
They can stop drinkin' 'n drivin'—Uber-sippin'.

When it comes to my name,
make no fuckin' mention.

This is how rumors get started.
This is how easily your reputation's discarded.
This is why I completely departed.
This is why I remain so g'damn guarded.

For moments like this,
when I'm full-on bombarded.

There's a knock—at the back door,
that I wasn't expectin'.

Two of my buddies have
surprisingly checked in.

They're the odd couple,
of impartial interjection.

They quickly make me well aware
of this visit's intention . . .

. . .'n I'm all like—hold up!

This is where I ask YOU a quick question:

Have you ever had your friends
set you up—for an intervention?

I have!
TODAY

Before I go any further,
there's somethin' that I don't
wanna fail to mention—to say . . .

A tree member's also the direct cause
of THIS dissension.

SURPRISE*—better yet—*DISMAY

This person's got a serious issue with me.
An undyin' need—to put me down.

That's always on full display.

So, I won't say they're here, too.
You can call it "notoriety prevention" . . . okay?

Movin' on . . .

The room is, now, over-flowin' with tension.
And the bullshit? It's quietly crept in.
Yeah, that's that shit I've already stepped in.

Can you smell what the chef is cheffin'?

I had a gut feelin' that you could.

Although I know that
their intentions were good . . .
they knew a lot less,
about the situation,
than I believe they really should.
In order to try to make amends
(between that person 'n me), in any/all likelihood.

Unless you've heard both sides,
our current relationship
could easily be misunderstood.

. . . And I'm tired of bein' the one
constantly defendin' my livelihood.

For once . . . just ONCE . . .

for ME . . .

I wish that somebody, anybody, else would.

My poetic thoughts
shouldn't lead to flo-etic shots
at ho-etic thots—from the neighborhood.

But, at any moment, they quite easily could.

If I wasn't fully prepared
for this impromptu meetin'.

. . . And the purpose of this meetin'
I'm wholeheartedly defeatin'.

'Cause they're unaware that I know
that THIS PERSON'S been spreadin' rumors
about me interweb cheatin'.
Due to me payin' the siblin'
of a mutual female FRIEND
what they deemed an
awkward "Wally-world" greetin' . . .

The truth is . . .
fuck if I could remember that kid's name,
so I kept it extremely discreet 'n
introduced her as my fiancée . . .
then went off on our way
to look for new basement seatin'.

Now, in return,
these two think that they're here
in order to repair
some minor despair,
based upon the watered-down

version of the situation they hear
every g'damn day in their ear . . .
of the same fictional stories
this person just keeps on repeatin'.

"They don't understand why
you're not speakin'."

So, once again, I break down
every single fuckin' lie.

While in my mind
I'm fully projectile geekin' . . .

I really don't owe anyone
any explanations as to why.
But, we're friends.
So, I have to try to defend myself, eye for eye,
against these false allegations, by 'n by.

Why?

Because I've NEVER, in my life,
been THAT type of guy.

I'M AS LOYAL AS THEY COME,
'TIL THE DAY THAT I DIE!

"Tell them nice fuckin' try."

. . . And with that, I bid those two
goodbye!

closes door

COUCH SESSIONS

By now you've probably
already asked yourself,

"How does he keep his sanity?"
(or somethin' of the like).

Well . . .
there's somethin'
soothingly therapeutic
that happens whenever
I profoundly write.

Allow me to share with you
a laughable li'l somethin' . . .
that I believe God had,
deliberately,
liberated me.

I needed some counselin',
as a direct result of
my dysfunctional family.

You see . . .
I've got a thoughtful therapist,
in my pants pocket.

I've been pocket-poolin'
my way through
strenuous sessions
of therapy.

Non-physically . . .
arguably.

You feelin' me?
NO, DONT!
At least not literally.
Figuratively . . .
okay!?
LET'S GO!

YES! He is up front,
'n straight forward.
NO filter.
Just basic instinct.

And he ALWAYS
wears protection
that's distinct . . .

He's learned the hard way
that keepin' it covered
is key to keepin' it safe
'n clean . . .

wink, wink

Oh, 'n it's black.
Not white,
nor pink.

Oh, woah . . .
wait, what!?

No . . . no . . . no . . .
I'm not referrin' to a
grower nor a shower,
not a monstrosity,
nor a miniscule
shrinky dink.

I should've made a
bold-faced prediction.

I knew exactly what
your perverse mind
would, piggishly, think.

'Cause . . .
I'm just talkin' 'bout my
discreetly-concealed
cellular, Note II.

My above-average,
while underpaid,
personal pocket shrink.

Y'freak.
This is the type of shit
that constantly clogs
my magnificent mind.

Whenever I'm not
dealin' with the drama,
in which I've been placed
in a circumstantial bind.

Yet, I always find
a wonderful way
to nonchalantly
peruse through it.

I stay on my . . .
#PoeticGrind

HIGH STAKES

I know that I believe in Heaven,
because at times I feel
like I'm finally ready t'go.

All of the warnin' signs are startin'
to become a crucial part of the show.

No more reason for procrastination.
No more rhyme in takin' it slow.

The clouds begin to take their shape,
in the form of a high stakes ca•si•no.

When the body's used up all its heartache,
the dealer of Life will collect
on your final roll.

They've been gamblin' with my name.
Karma's got me devilin' for their soul.

Their IQ is their claim to fame.
They should have been smart enough to fold.

Here's where I place "my all-in bet"
that they'll forever question "all my intent."

The one thing that they'll neither never get
is that they're more alike
than either of 'em will admit.

Although, I no longer blame
the leaf-like element
f'makin' me feel so damn irrelevant.

The seed they birthed that wasn't meant.
"We should have placed you up for adoption!"
once graced a text that they'd sent.

It's time f'me to collect your unpaid debt.
I'm deviant . . .

Sometimes I wish that I could vent.
Without the ridicule 'n ill judgment.
I'm their floor mat!?
Screw that shit!
If I wasn't so intelligent,
I would pull some hella shit.
Drag their ass atop the tallest bridge,
'n throw us both off the top
of that son'bitch,
just for the fuckin' hell of it.
I've no more reason to budget.
My time with them is all but spent.
I'm no longer payin' social rent,
to a sidekick that doesn't compliment,
the lifestyle that I represent.
There are just some things
that you can't repent.
Like each outlandish lie
they've ever shed.
If you believe that bullshit,
you've been misled.
I'm over it.
This thought is DEAD!

Murdered . . .

I know that I believe in Heaven,
because at times I feel like
I'm finally ready t'go . . .

SUICIDE ON MY MIND

I thought about
“hangin’ out”—in the basement.

But I didn’t want t’be
a “noose-ance”
by causin’ a scene.

I thought about
“lightin’ a fire under my ass”
with a match
‘n some kerosene.

But I don’t want to
bring harm to our home . . .
that’s a bit too extreme.

I thought about
consumin’ a nice, fat, juicy steak,
covered with a scrumptious
rat seasonin’.

But I didn’t want to
go out that way . . .
at least that was my
self-reasonin’.

After a lifetime of sober livin’,
these two chauffeurs
are drivin’ my (straight-edge) ass to drink.

They’ve been arguin’—for over an hour.

When they’re done,

I'ma need to speak to a clinical shrink.

I never thought they'd come to this . . .

Tit for tat.
Blow by blow.
This shit fuckin' stinks.

Never been about quittin'
but they're seriously pushin' me
towards the brink.

One of these times,
I'ma think it too far . . .
'n actually follow through
on these urges—I control.

Until then . . .
I'ma keep patchin' up each,
'n every, drama-filled hole.

That is 'til, into my own ditch,
I plummit . . .
'n lifelessly sink.

It's all about contemplatin' suicide . . .

while gettin' drunk
off of these monotonous thoughts
that I over-strenuously think.

THIS is what it's like—t'be rome.

THIS is what lies,
behind the blue eyes,
that can so elegantly compromise,

ANY circumstance—that I internalize,
in order to prevent the outward cries,
that I keep bottled up inside—like a drink.

“But his life is so perfect!”

If that’s the way it looks . . .
‘cause I ever-so-calmly smile ‘n wink,

then, I guess rome’s a hell of a lot stronger
than any of you motherfuckers think.

Best believe . . .

JUST WHAT THE DOCTOR ORDERED

They forced me to
drop this serious shit.
This delirious hit.
On a conspiracy bit.
In the best way
that only I could see fit . . .

By unleashin’ the demon,
that I’ve always kept confined.

How can they possibly
threaten to sue me,
for givin’ new life
to all of the miscellaneous
memories that they’d
expected just to die
in the back of my mind?

I needed them resurrected.

I needed all of them
pieced together . . .
FULLY combined.

They have no legal say,
over any of the pieces,
that I've verbally sewn
together to form THIS
"Mental Frankenstein."

Now I'm fittin' to release
this monsta—to the streets!

I'ma gladly hand 'em my
freedom of speech.

'Cause, ain't nobody
unwillingly takin' mine!

If they wanted to obtain
the rights to my thoughts,
then they should've had
my fuckin' brain patented.

But I can tell you
exactly the fuck
why THAT ENDED.

Quite simply . . .
I own the exclusive rights,
to every fuckin' neuron that I hit.

Every single word
that I've been spittin'

is elaborately written,
in the lab, with a
purpose to each fit.

There's a science to this shit.

In order for you to
fully understand
where my thoughts keep goin',
I need you to know
exactly where the hell they've been.

"What makes rome the person
that so many call their friend?"

I'ma keep it real.
This is me.
I refuse to pretend.

My heart's been through
the frickin' ringer.

It's constantly on the
g'damn mend.

I've held my life together
with so many
multitudes of stitches . . .
my seedhood alone
should be condemned.

It's gone way beyond
the point where
I'm so fuckin' tired
of constantly havin'
my feelings re-hemmed.

I know that I'm far
from bein' perfect.
I've made my fair
share of mistakes.

Someday I'ma make
everythin' straight.

I don't care how long it takes.

In the meantime,
I'ma sit here and wait.

I've got some time—to contemplate.

Best believe,
I'm a firm believer in fate.

It's a concept that I used to hate.

I'm impatient.
I don't usually like to wait.

But it'll all be worth it,
once this monsta
makes its way through
the United States . . .

I expect all to speculate . . .
I'm fully prepared to wait.
Make 'em great.

TIPPED KING

It's been a little over a year,
since the last time we spoke.
Things appear to (finally)
be settlin' down.

I've found some peace 'n comfort,
which is both upliftin' 'n profound.

I hear that you're still askin' people
what's goin' on with me, though.

I think, real soon, that question
could go viral—world-renowned.

Only this time you'll be on the receivin' end.
And that question—might just be turnt around.

As you see, I've taken some time to clear my mind.
Damn . . . I like the way that sounds.
It's been a minute—since I felt this free.
Sixty seconds—without shackled verbs to nouns.

I must admit, that there have been instances
where I thought to myself
that you were homeward bound.
That's usually the point where my
phone would ring.
Ring . . .
RING!

But the cell doesn't make a sound.

This time a "slap in the face" by reality,

is what reminds me why we can no longer
stand together—on common ground.

Your hands can no longer reach.
No more "lessons" needed to teach.
No more practice.
No more preach.

Better yet:
no more clingin', like a leech,
of a pussy-whipped seed to a peach.

Throw away the fruit . . . I beseech!
That's one final "FUCK YOU!"—
by my middle finger of speech.

Okay.
Now last but certainly NOT least . . .
there's no need for you to frown.
You can still kiss the ring.
But you've really gotta stop
eyeballin' the crown.

It's awkward
. . . and
kinda weird.

drops pen

GRAND•IOSE

Yet another thought I share,
with tears—runnin' down my face.

One right after another.

It's a fuckin' downhill race.

I get kind of emotional
when I reflect upon
all of the time
that's been misplaced.

Such a g'damn disgrace.

Yet, if not for them,
there'd be no me.
It's some crazy shit . . .
that DNA.

The females, I knew both.
But the males . . .
due to different circumstances,
they'd already gone away.

The one, on that side,
passed away pre-rome.

The one, on this side,
ran away from home.

Neither of them
have I ever known.

But only God knows
how many times I reflect
'n wish that I had.

How much would our
upbringin' have changed,

if either (or both)
had been raised
by their . . .

Maybe I think too much.
Maybe I've no such luck.
Maybe I just shouldn't give a fuck.

If I've any fucks left,
to give.

Damn, shit, fuck . . .
this life—I've been made to live.

I've already done thrown
myself a pity party.

(Okay, I've thrown myself quite a few.)

I'm sayin' though:
Wouldn't you have done the same,
if you'd been through
all of the shit—that I've been through?

Take a minute to mull it over.
Hell, I'll give you a few . . .

Maybe I'm just bein' hard on myself.
My mind is a dangerous place, to fret.

Over-consumed
by a multitude of thoughts
that, at times, even I don't get.

Maybe my expectations were
too high—for this guy . . .

who's always in my face,
even though we've never met.

Shit,
we've never even looked each other
in the eyes . . .
I often wonder if, when he dies,
he'll have harbored the same regret.

I try not to hate.
But I do despise the relationships
that I'll never get.

From one that passed away,
'n another that just up 'n jet.

Such a godawful feelin',
that's always on my
saddened mind . . .
even though I say that
"I'm all set."

LOSIN' BATTLE

Got upended
Yep, unfriended.
Not offended.
No amendment.

. . . And why the hell
should there be one?

I'm not chasin' anyone
that decides to turn

their backs on me.

They're done . . .

3
2
1
RUN!

I've got a dangerous weapon
concealed—in my pants pocket.

I reach my hand inside
'n "cock it."

She's pleadin',
"No, rome!
You can't!
Please, drop it!"

She doesn't want
this released.
But it's already too late.

I'm already fully engaged
in the process.

It feels too good—to stop it.

I don't give a single shit,
if I profit.

The writin' of pain,
on my cellular device . . .
no feelin' can compare,
nor top it.

Until you've tried it,
you shouldn't knock it.

For years,
I've worn these fears
around my neck,
like a g'damn locket.

I've been stranglin'
my thoughts with this
chain-link noose . . .
every time I shackle 'em,
to the back of my mind,
'n lock it.

But that's all changed,
since I picked my brain,
'n threw away the key
to this docket.

You see,
last night I prayed to God . . .
on bended knee—for some leniency.

I apologized for prayin'
to Him so infrequently.

So conveniently . . .

Lately we haven't spoken,
like we should.

I haven't done everythin'
towards our relationship
that we both know I could.

Since it seems as though
I'm only prayin' for things of good.

It's been a while
since I'd asked His forgiveness
for my mistakes.

I fully understand . . .
the Good Lord gives
as well as
the Good Lord takes.

It would appear that
I've been askin' for too much.

Between my heart,
my anxiety,
our baby,
'n such.

That somewhere I've lost touch
of what is truly important.

Makin' the most of opportunities.
That's important.

Together, she and I are strong.
We've built this unbreakable bond.
We have the strength to carry on.
We should be thankful
that He gave us the opportunity.

Life—of any kind—is an opportunity.

If you'd like to walk away from me,
here's your opportunity.

"Forgive me, Lord,
for I have sinned.
Forgive them, Lord,
for they caught wind."

That I'm writin' fire—
about committed sins.

And . . . in a game of wrongs,
nobody wins.

WANNABE

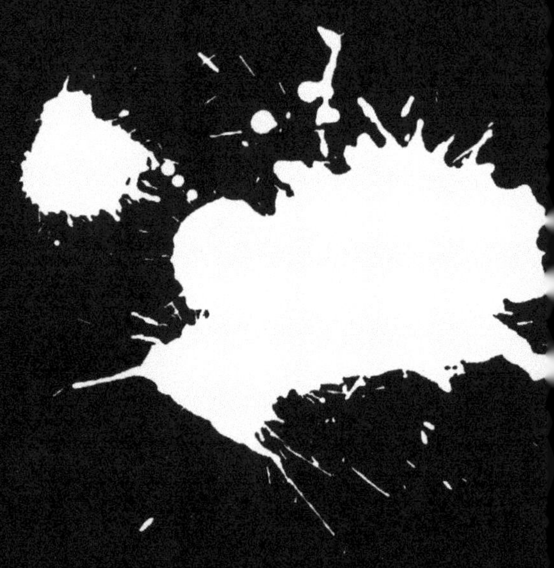

I just wanna touch
your freakin' heart,
with every sentence
that I write.

I'm a wannabe . . .
I wanna be your
first thought
in the mornin',
'n your last thought
every night.

I wanna be the one
that gives you
the courage
not to walk away,
but stand your ground
and forever fight . . .

for everythin' that
you've ever believed in.

For everythin' that
you've known deep down,
inside your heart,
is right.

I wanna be the answer,
the next time you're faced
with a difficult question.

I wanna be your
support system durin'
the saddest moments
of self-expression.

I wanna be the positivity,
in those moments of weakness,
that lifts you back up
from your feelings
of depression.

I wanna be your
inspiration towards
that progression.

I wanna be the
outstretched hand
you look to hold.

I wanna be wrapped
around your fingers,
in that hand,
whenever they bend
to fold.

I wanna be the one
that sits with you,

in silence,
when there are no words
that can be said.

I wanna be there
whenever you feel the need,
to talk about it,
or just to clear your head.

I could go on 'n on forever.

In fact,
I could go on speakin'
metaphorically . . .

'cause
I wanna be the one
that writes the air,
that you inhale,
to breathe.

That way every time
you read my words,
you exhale all of the love
that was written for you,
to see.

I guess what I'm sayin' is,
I wanna be your everythin' . . .

the same way you've been
everythin'—to ME!

#DUMBASS

I've poured my blood
through the quill.
Imposin' ill will.
As if it were travelin'—
through a vein.

On this paper,
I'm hemorrhagin' pain.

Like a needle punctured
directly into my brain.
The objective is to
intravenously drain
all of these memories
that are drivin' me absolutely nuts!

I'm literally goin' insane.
EVERYONE is to blame.
My emotions are runnin' amok.
Wreakin' havoc, 'n chaos, 'n such.
EVERYTHIN' about bein' related to you . . .
just FUCKIN' SUCKS!

Which is crazy.
Because I love you, so frickin' much.

Believe it, or not . . .
my heart's been inconsolably touched.

I'm happy.
I'm sad.
I'm angrier than mad.
I can't move on.

My feelings have been boxed . . .
But, in a rut—I'm mentally stuck.

Unfortunately . . .
the scenario has always been the same.
I'll forever be their "claim to fame."

As long as I'm alive,
they'll continue spreadin' lies.
They make me so sick to my stomach,
at times—I could chuck.

They can't help but to
bring up my name.
Whether negative or positive . . .
it'll never change.
"J.E. rome this . . ."
"rome that . . ."
"Jay the other . . ."

WHAT THE FUCK!?

You've no idea, the level of lies,
'n nonsense they say.
To anyone that will listen,
'n throw some attention—their way.

•1 "He's been single for six years.
I think he might be gay."

•2 "He's been datin' all these girls.
He's playin' games—that playa plays."

•3 "All of those witty things he says,
and all of those poems you like?
He gets them from a secret website.

He can't really write."

Oh, wait.
I almost forgot.
This one is a gem—of a beauty.

•4 "His female friend asked him if she could
become my Facebook friend.
To which he responded quite rudely,
'You're not allowed t'be friends with him.
He's a pirate, who tries to steal all my booty.'"
(Reference back to •1.)

#DUMBASS

MISERY LOVES COMPANY

This thought stems from a situation
where two adults have had a fallin' out,
'n their seeds assume some of that blame.
Guilty, by association.
That's the name of this game.

Sometimes the social networks
get me feelin' a certain way.
It's difficult raisin' grownups.
I don't appreciate the childish (online)
personas these posers attempt to portray.

This leaf hasn't associated with me,
in such a long period of time,
that she probably thinks
they still call me "J."

I really don't give two shits
about anythin' she currently has to say.
But what the fuck has she got to gain
by condescendingly typin'
around my name—either way?

I know she saw my comment(s).
She's been replyin'
beneath them—all g'damn day.

Maybe she just felt the need
to patronize me today . . .

she's been tryin' to goad me to say
somethin' (ANYTHING) her way

by includin' them two frauds,
in these fucked-up games they play.
Spreadin' fake love to a seed,
who she's never given the time of day.

At least not in person—anyway.

The tree's biggest turncoat.
I'm not surprised, they'd shown no shame.
They'd turn their back on their own shoulders,
if they felt they had somethin' to gain.

"I love you this, I love you that."
You're all so fuckin' lame.

Your internet love is as believable
as that business's sudden rise to fame.
Or so they claim.

Many times I've been a few keystrokes away

from callin' their ass out—in that public forum.
I've formed a hatred towards these types of
non-interactive exchanges—I absolutely abhor 'em.

Instead I've continually bitten my tongue.
For years, I just tried to ignore 'em.

It's a damn good thing for them
that I still have respect for their seed
(about whom they once raved 'n ranted).
I'm not talkin' 'bout the weeds,
which they transported 'n transplanted.

'Cause they saved them
from my original thought,
in which I angrily chanted.

I had to take a minute—to rethink.
'Cause once I think 'em,
the original thought
can't be recanted.

But you have to realize that
none of this would have ever been thought,
had they not—taken my silence for granted.

YOU HAVE NO IDEA

What do you know about
bein' read your last rights,
'n wishin' that you had died first?

What do you know about
bein' told that you were a mistake,

an unwanted birth?

What do you know about
hidin' the pain,
so as not to give them the satisfaction
of your hurt?

What do you know
about valuin' life,
while questionin'
your own self-worth?

What do you know
about cryin' yourself to sleep,
over family disputes—each night?

What do you know
about puttin' on a happy face,
to hide the fact that you aren't alright?

What do you know
about givin' up hope,
once you've lost your
willingness to fight?

What do you know
about comin' to terms
with your family's
hatred towards you,
'n thinkin' to yourself,
"Tonight's gonna be the night!"?

What do you know
about scavengin' holes,
'n plottin' your own demise?

What do you know
about cryin' for help,
when the tears are bein' cried
on the inside?

What do you know,
about feelin' helplessly alone,
'n wishin' that somebody could read
your mind?

What do you know
about plannin' your future,
by considerin' urns or caskets?

What do you know
about writin' your will,
'n delegatin' all of your assets?

Besides what you see,
'n whatever you've been told . . .

what do you know
about bein' rome?

For real, though . . .

FAILURE IS AN OPTION

Obviously, I can't tell you everythin'.
Neither of us have that kind of time.

What I have tried t'do, however . . .
is give you an idea of how it was,
growin' up for me 'n mine—in rhyme.

These are MY perceptions.
So, you can save your misconceptions
of the obstacles that I've had to climb.

Until you've walked a mile in my shoes,
please, don't judge my path.

From the bulk of my tree,
I've already (unwillingly)
endured THAT wrath.

But no one in this world can tell me
what I can, or cannot, think.

MYSELF INCLUDED.

I have no control over my thoughts.
But I do have a say over exactly
how they get redistributed.

You can say whatever you want.
You don't have to agree.
You're entitled to your opinion,
one-hundred percent.

This is solely my explanation
of another event . . .
in which I feel the need
to release from my head.

Even though they say some things
are better off bein' left unsaid.

I can't take these thoughts
with me to my grave when I'm dead.

I've been keepin' some skeletons
in my closet for a rainy day.

I've never been close to perfect.
What can I say?

Okay . . .

deep breath

My life is all or nothin'.
There's no stoppin' in the middle . . .
half-way.

I have to push all the way through.

OCD had me buggin' out,
on every single minuscule move.

I kept thinkin' to myself,
"What have you really got to lose!?"

Everythin' . . .

Y'see . . . I'd been contemplatin' suicide,
since the ripe old age of nine.

This is but another of such incidents . . .
the likes of this—that you'll find.

If it's at all possible
to hate someone you love,
I'm teeterin' that fine line.

I really can see past their bullshit.
They say that "love is blind."

But I've got a well-trained eye.

They like to wait until
my back is fully turned,
before they muster up
the guts—to come hunt me.

They're all scared to
approach me face to face.
No balls to physically confront me.

I've tried to hide from my current.
I've always hidden from my past.
I could hide from my future.
But not for long does THAT ever last.

Right now—I'm talkin' 'bout my past.
This outrageously persistent past.
By this incident of the past,
my mind is constantly bein' harassed.

Sometimes I think on some ridiculousness.
But on those uncouth thoughts . . .
I thought I'd never act.

I can't control these urges.
They often lack morals, 'n tact.

I take no ownership over the content,
while ridin' those emotional spats.

I've no choice, but to hop on board.
I've got a non-refundable,
infinite, season pass.

Which leads me to the first time a doctor

diagnosed me with depression.
I was like, "That's not really news, to me."

I've dealt my whole life with
bein' obsessive compulsive.
Depression coincides with my O.C.D.

I've always been like,
"Love me, for me—or set me free."
(All or nothin'—is the way that I was raised t'be.)

Whenever one door closed,
I've kicked my way through
every memory that my
brain so accurately drew up.

I'm so frickin' stressed out, 'n it shows.
I'm constantly tryin' to show my leaves
that I'm not just a fuckin' screw-up!

Especially since I failed at yet another attempt . . .
I still can't do it . . .
all those pills . . .
I panicked, finger gagged, 'n threw up.

Why am I always the one,
forced to swallow the pain,
'n all of their pride?

I could fill a porcelain toilet,
with all of the pent-up bullshit
that I keep hidden inside.

Or, in this case, pharmaceutical spew up.

Up until this point in my life

I'd seen more turnt backs
than smilin' faces.

I'd felt more knives,
than warm embraces.

I'd suffered more let downs,
than supportive praises.

. . . And this third attempt,
at endin' my life—jus' totally blew up.

There it is . . .
once again, I'm late-night-feelin' suicidal . . .
lookin' to talk to somebody . . .

anybody . . .
who up!?

FRICTION

Always holier-than-thou, bitchin'.
Seems like they're non-stop moanin', 'n pissin'.
Must be part of their lack of memory, contradiction.
I don't need the friction.

I'ma hide out—in my safe place . . .
head down,
eyes closed,
hands coverin' my face.

Always insecurely bitchin'.
Seems like they're on another vindictive mission.
Must be part of their failed relationship predisposition.

I don't need the friction.

I'ma hide out—in my safe place . . .
head down,
eyes closed,
hands coverin' my face.

Always money problems, bitchin'.
Seems like they've picked up another prescription.
Must be part of their condition.
I don't need the friction.

I'ma hide out—in my safe place . . .
head down,
eyes closed,
hands coverin' my face.

Always alcohol-induced bitchin'.
Seems like they've got that day-off blurred vision.
Must be part of their addiction.
I don't need the friction.

I'ma hide out—in my safe place . . .
head down,
eyes closed,
hands coverin' my face.

I'm in way over my head,
with all of their personal conflictions.
This isn't the environment to raise kids in.
Don't no seed have the time for all their bitchin'.

I'ma hide out—in my safe place . . .
head down,
eyes closed,
hands coverin' my face.

I've developed a nervous twitch in
both of my eyes—they keep on switchin'.
Sometimes I shut 'em both—in hopes, I'm wishin',
for someone to rescue us—from this conviction.

I'ma hide out—in my safe place . . .
head down,
eyes closed,
hands coverin' my face.

I hate bein' caught up in this position,
which is why I've made it my mission
to move on with my life 'n transition
myself away from any/all opposition.

I'ma ride out—of my safe place . . .
head high, eyes open, smile coverin' my face.

Deuces!

AA

"Yo, yo, yo!
What it IS?
What it DO?
What it BE like?
I can't call it . . ."

What is THIS?
What a FOOL!
What is FREE life?

Alcoholic . . .

Shit,
he's been thrown
out of the **WILL**,
more times than **JACK** . . .
(as a matter of fact)
he's always been known
to fall out—of their good **GRACE**.

Then again . . .

he's also been known
to have been thrown
out of their home,
against his WILL 'n GRACE.

Sometimes a liquid dinner
is all that it really takes.

"Lou-dummy."

Words of uttered disgrace . . .
(or apropos—in this case).
Screamed aloud—by an infant
who already knows their place
in the family dynamics . . .
that fall in between alcoholic traits,
'n the favorite seed, "What's-its-face . . ."

'Cause

they pledged allegiance
to the nag
who divided the state—of our tree.
And to the redundant
bitch which stands
one abomination

under fraud,
('n despicable)
with bastardly
injustice.
Poor call.

Fuck if anyone's surprised,
by this never-endin' squall.

Fuck if it didn't cause
his "all-out" withdrawal.

Fuck if that leaf's been sober,
durin' any of their seedhood . . .
*NO, their livelihood—OVERALL.

It's safe to say—that ninety percent
of their fucked-up upbringin'
was riddled—by alcohol.

From the time that
he could fuckin' crawl . . .
all the way through
every belligerent, drunken brawl.
Shit, he remembers them ALL.

. . . And TRUST HIM—there were a lot!

Although, he couldn't count
the number of beatings that he'd caught.

Each 'n every time
those g'damn beers were bought . . .
that's the exact number of times,
with them, he's consequently fought.

While,
solitude is the lifestyle he sought.
Ingratitude is the attitude beers brought.
Subdued is his ass from the whoopings he caught.

Fuck alcoholism—'n the ensuin' onslaught.

He's NEVER drinkin' it . . .
not a single fuckin' drop.

Especially after they tried to fight him
over a TICKLE ME ELMO
that he kept in his bedroom
as a fuckin' bed prop.

When does this nonsense stop!?

FIGHTIN' IRISH

Lately I've been thinkin'
a ton—about our pasts.

It's become more than apparent
that you 'n I walk opposite paths.

It's been a bumpy road,
between us,
to say the very least.

I feel like we butt heads—an awful lot
'cause you tend not
to practice what you preach.

I can't tell you how many times,

I've wished that you could just
set your pride aside—'n teach.

But you've always been the type
to want to feel needed—despite
keepin' all of your knowledge
far enough out of my reach.

Basically, you've been withholdin'
an abundance of pertinent deets . . .
(that statement applies to both
personal, 'n physical, feats).

Although, I'm more hung up—on the personal.
If I'm tellin' the absolute truth.

You sold your soul—to the Devil
in an exchange
that I deem uncouth . . .

when you broke the pact,
to have each other's backs,
in order t'be able to spend
more time with THEIR youth.

Don't you ever get it twisted.
I still have the texted proof.
Shit's got me steady trippin'
over your conundrum . . .

hell, I've been tryin' to solve it, too.

I read the letter that you wrote,
when you were younger,
the other night.

You were once so proud
of your new title, ‘n
the position that you were
about to acquire—am I right?

Yeah,
I could sense the level of “excitement”
in the words that you chose to write.

But somewhere along the way,
you seem to have lost sight.

You ‘n I, we once actually
used t’be really tight.

Now it just seems like
we barely even communicate.

All we do is argue,
bicker,
‘n fight.

And that’s when we’re actually
speakin’ to each other, without spite.

Now they have your presence
active in their lives,
while me (‘n mine) are
forced to suffer through.

Hell,
I couldn’t even address you properly,
as I’ve always been known t’do.

I can’t refer to you
by your name,

since you threatened that, if I did,
you'd immediately sue.

How's that for a big
"Hey, rome, SCREW YOU"!?

Thanks a lot.
I fuckin' love you, too!

I know that came off
as bein' sarcastic . . .
'cause that's the way
I intended it to.

But it's true.
I really, wholeheartedly, do . . .

no matter what happens
between us.

No matter how far
we become estranged.

No matter what THEY say,
I mean US.

No matter what's said,
or been said in exchange . . .

GROUNDHOG DAY

His story is
her story when
history repeats itself.

I couldn't have said it any better,
if I had said it myself.

His story
IS
her story
when
history
REPEATS itself.

I couldn't have said it any better,
if I had said it myself.

HIS story
is HER story
when HISTORY repeats ITSELF.

I couldn't have said it any better,
if I had said it myself.

OH WAIT . . . WAIT . . .
I just did . . . did.

God forbid . . . bid . . .
I'm morbid . . . bid . . .
while he hid . . . hid . . .
off the grid . . . grid . . .
like a kid . . . kid . . .
from Madrid . . . drid . . .

"Where•In•The•World•Is . . ."

HOLD UP

I can feel his presence,
lurkin' from his burrow (hole).

Watchin' over me,
in search of intel,
as if he were a thorough mole.

He'll lie—about an early spring—
'cause his shadow WILL NOT SHOW.

"PUNKsaSCRAWNY Build" I'ma call 'em,
'n expect several feet of snow . . .
covered bullshit
as their celly convos blow . . .
out of proportion
like I know—you know—we know
they tend t'do.

It's happened a time,
or quite a few.

It's happened a time,
or quite a few.

It's happened . . .

WARDROBE MALFUNCTION

I'd give you the shirt
off of my back.

The heart,
on the sleeve?

Oh, yes.
That's INCLUDED!

Until I catch you
stockpilin' my wardrobe.

Do that shit,
'n your ass—it's SECLUDED!

I really don't like
bein' taken advantage of.

From this particular thought,
NOBODY'S EXCLUDED!

I mean,
do you know anyone
who likes bein' taken
for granted?

That leaf's always got
their fuckin' hand out.

Why can't they just be thankful,
for all that they've (already)
been handed?

Nothin' is ever good enough.

I couldn't possibly fulfill
all of the prerequisites
that they've demanded.

Nor could that one.
Nor them.
Or anyone else.
If, in that uncompromisin' position,
they (themselves) had landed.

This is usually the point
where I start gettin' anxious, 'n quit.

Where most of my anxiety
stems from—legit.

The point where our relationship
turnt to relation-dog-shit.

When I begin to
feel myself losin' control,
it's time to split.

The cause of my disdain.
I could no longer refrain,
from dealin' with the pain
on the left side—of my chest.

Always on my brain.
Drivin' me insane.
Never, mentally, do I rest.

The only way I gain
is to directly confront the main
source of all this shame.
I must confess.

I hold myself to blame.
To no one else will I complain.
I remain suppressed.

When wishin' that they'd change,
they never fuckin' change.

They're
not

gonna
change.

Why do I continuously stress!?

TRISOMY 18

This pregnancy's got me twisted,
more than I could ever depict.

I can't wrap my brain around
the outcome that
these doctors are attemptin'
to predict.

I try to separate my thoughts
far enough away
from my beliefs
whenever the two conflict.

I've become a master peacemaker.
But this situation's got me licked.

You see . . .
they have a very difficult time
comminglin' together.

Each other,
they (almost always) contradict.

T'be perfectly clear,
with certainty—I'm a strict,
yet firm, believer
in God,

in Heaven,
in the "afterlife" . . .
but who are we to elaborate on
the course of an unwritten script?

I'm jus' sayin',
I often catch myself thinkin',
"What if . . ."

Okay,
lately, I'm always thinkin',
"What if . . ."

I.e., what if death is
bein' consumed
by a dark, black, quiet abyss?
GONE . . .
abruptly,
albeit swift.

One day
. . . our eyesight's no longer lit.
. . . our ears go silent.
. . . our heart stops beatin'.
. . . our lungs stop breathin'.
. . . our brain goes clear.
. . . all at once, these realities hit.

No more scenes.
No more sounds.
No more feelings.
No more thoughts.
No more tastes.
No more nothin'.

. . . Shit.

Absolutely NOTHIN'.
We're nonexistent.
That's it.

What if . . .
when we die,
that's literally fuckin' IT!?

The end.
No más.
Once our body's given up,
life's over.
No afterlife.
No more anythin'.
Done.
Gone.
QUIT!

Let's improvise some shit . . .
• Black out the room.
• Turn everythin' off.
• Close your eyes.
• Cover your ears.
• DON'T THINK AT ALL.
• Don't move.
• Just sit.

Now take a second to,
in the utmost literal form,
think about it . . .

[PURGATORY]

What if, RIGHT NOW, every second
is ALL OF THE LIFE
that we're EVER gonna get?

If you're at all like me,
right now I'd be willin' to bet
that you're also thinkin':

"Fuck!
I could die
with a shit ton
of regret!"

Which brings me
right back to my beliefs,
'n once again I think,
"What if . . ."

What if God needs an angel?
And that angel
is the gift
that He bestowed
upon her 'n I.

Who am I to question
His existence . . .

His decisions . . .

Who am I to question
WHY!?

What if our baby boy's to serve
a greater purpose?

Maybe that's what
this baby's birth is.

Maybe God
(all along) has had

preconceived intentions
for him to fly . . .

I take great pride
in bein' a strong,
chivalrous guy.

I know I've got t'be strong
for her sake,
whenever we're eye to eye.

I hold my composure,
'n keep my head held high.

Yet, I can't help
but to break down
'n secretively cry.

I can't come to grips
with the possibility of
never knowin' my seed,
no matter how hard I try.

I DON'T WANT OUR UNBORN SON
TO DIE . . .

I'm not ready . . .
to place him into the
outstretched hands
up in the sky.

I still have hope . . .

SOMETHIN' BORROWED

This is the type of craziness
that keeps me fucked-up inside.
Another fuckin' rabbit hole,
opened up by a "Wisconsinite."

I've run out of people to rely on.
I've squandered all of my inner sanctums to hide.
My entire life I've been proud t'be one thing.
My whole ancestral perspective has been lie after lie.
All these years without havin' the faintest idea . . .

AHHHHHHHHH, WHAT IN THE FUCK!

At what point was someone gonna tell US, them 'n I,
that those weren't the original leaves
that THEIR leaf may have had?

Oh, wait . . .
you didn't know, either?
Well, that makes two of us.
This shit gets me so fuckin' pissed off.
I'm beyond the point of feelin' bad.

sillE rome.

Once again, you've been misled—it's a fad.

When they said, "You should've been adopted,"
they must've meant just like . . . **egads**

This thought, alone, has always left me sad.
But this new news has me ragin' mad!
Or confused?

Err, I don't even know how to feel anymore.

Who was he, before?!

Keltin kin.
It's meltin' in.
Not in my hands . . . but under my skin.
My DNA, it came from him.
But I have minimal knowledge
as to where he's been.

Who am I?

CONUNDRUM

How many times
should you forgive 'n forget,
before it's time
to stop forgivin' 'n forgettin'?

How many times
can you be forewarned
(of future regrets)
before you lose that fear
of what you "could be" regrettin'?

I go back 'n forth
with the way I feel that family
problems should be worked out.

I like to put together puzzles,
to see where the missin' pieces
have all come about.

There seems t'be
a hole in every story.
Which gives me this constant,
reasonable doubt.

In the back of my mind,
I think it hard to find,
that their intentions are sincere, or devout.

I used to always look for the good—in people.
Now, I find myself (subconsciously)
waitin' for the bad—to come out.

I hate that I've become this mistrustin'.
I've been fucked over so often
it's flat-out disgustin'.

They make me so fuckin' angry!
Now I'm cussin'.
It seems like, lately, I'm always friggin' cussin'.

Another thought that I shouldn't
have t'be discussin'.

They tell me,
"rome, it's not worth the time.
Stop your fussin'."

Like I'ma pretend t'be some
type of an ignorant immigrant:
"DAS NO ME! ME NOT KNOW NUSSIN'"!?

tilts head
shrugs shoulders

The fuck outta here . . .

with that nonsense—you're gushin'.

Them problems—shit is real.
Those relatives—lack appeal.
The facts—same ol' spiel.
That hurt—a constant feel.
These words—how I deal.
This process—needed to heal.

Forgive 'n forget?
Fear of regret?

Prayin' for solutions seems so surreal.
Towards problems I need resolved . . .
each 'n every time I kneel.

That is . . .
until the next
(and there's always a next)
family ordeal.

Sad.

MAYBE

Maybe, one day,
we'll each see Heaven.
Assumin' we both
make it there.
Them 'n I.

Maybe God will
be our mediator,
in a radiant conference room,

up in the bright blue sky.

Maybe when we all
sit down together,
they'll be asked to explain
their side.

Maybe then they'll have
no other choice
but to understand exactly why
we could never see eye to eye.

In other words . . .
maybe. Just maybe.
God will finally get them to eat
their portion of that
humble pie.

Maybe then THEY won't be
allowed to leave that table,
until every friggin' morsel
they're made to try.

And maybe they'll be made
to wash it down
with a nice, tall glass
of ice-cold pride.

Then maybe they'll
finally get a taste
of humble pie,
while swallowin'
pummeled pride.

'Cause here on Earth,
there's not a fuckin' chance.

The Good Lord knows
how hard I've tried.

Right, wrong, or indifferent,
they only know one side.

"THEIR way
or no way"
is a tough way
to navigate your way
through this wayward life.

E.I. E.I. O.O.

It's an unspoken rule
that we don't drop names.

Whether it was J.P. or m'dude E . . .
the rule remains—one in the same.

But I've gotta show 'em both love,
outside of the game . . .
in jest, of course.
Despite of all the "fame."

Growin' up—at an early age.
Home was a mess,
'n I was enraged.

I'd been blamin' myself,
for "grown folks'" mistakes.

If I'd ever known anythin',
I was certain of two things.

Somethin' had to give . . .
'n I'd do whatever it takes . . .
to free my depressed mind,
for goodness' sake.

The House of Friendliness—in Worcester.
THAT was the place.

Home away from home.
Shelter. Most days, our savin' grace.

Where J.P. asked me to ball,
'n began to change
the path of my life . . .
while teachin' me plays.

Both for basketball 'n life.
A debt I'd love to—someday—repay.

(Side note: This was around the As,
but well before the Jays.

I owe him so much . . .
so much more—than a "thanks."

I'm jus' glad he's now with the Mets.
'Cause I could neva root for—the Yanks.)

The court quickly became
my sanctuary—'n I took center stage.

By the time I reached high school,
I no longer felt caged.

Like a dog—off its leash,
released from its chains.

I left everythin'—on that floor
every single time that I played.

Releasin' pent-up stress, on defense.
More so when I'd dunk, for some fame.
While tryin' my best to impress
every single person that came . . .
to see me "go off"
while hidin' from the pain.

Basketball, to me,
is so much MORE than a game.

It's a brotherhood,
which means EVERYTHIN'—to me.

When I think of the term
"BROTHERHOOD,"
I think of one word: LOYALTY.

And to me . . .
a brother doesn't need t'be royal
t'be treated like he's royalty.

He's just gotta be LOYAL,
like m'brother "E."

And when it comes to bein' fam,
E's been more like a brother,
than I could ever ask 'im t'be.

It's always nothin' but love,
when we conversate over 'n above,
of our mutual feelings for basketball . . .
'n, more importantly, family—respectfully.

Especially . . .
when I crack jokes about age—ancestrally.

You see . . .
my bro E.I.'s been ballin'
since before Bubba chucked
his first three.

Yeah . . .
that's a play on words,
from MA to Philly.

Off the top of my head,
no practice, in need.

That's right.

We talkin' 'bout practice . . . practice, indeed.

A.I. or E.I.,
neva made much
of a difference—to me.

I'll always celebrate my brother
from another mother
like no other—as a local celebrity.

Not "Answer" with an A.
We talkin' 'bout "Excellence" with an E.

"E.I.!"

To my brother 2-4,
from your brother 3-3:
I appreciate you, fam!
Wholeheartedly.

STILL DWELLIN'

I've reached my limit for cavin' in.
"The bigger man" no longer exists.

One day I woke up tired of that role,
'n began to pack up everyone's bullshit.
Filled several trash bags
with their nonsense.
Now on a curb,
that shit can sit.

With two fingers raised proudly, in the air,
I walked away from all of it.
Never again to return.
No more will I endure.

I FUCKIN' QUIT!

You see . . .
although I'm alive,
I've yet to start livin'.
Everyone else always comes first.

My nature is to give,
yet I've a hard time forgivin'.
Pardon my sudden outburst.

BUT . . .

when you said what you meant to say,
did you really mean it?

Y'sent it through that hateful text.
For you, that's just some routine shit.

I was the only one for whom it was intended.
But not the only one who'd seen it.

I should've been adopted?
You sound like a giant penis!

No need for us to agree to disagree,
'cause we're always in disagreement.

I'ma dead this thought, now.
I've already spent enough time
dwellin' on it—bereavement.

B.Y.O.T. (LIGHT)/P.S.A.

Guess what!?

I'm throwin' myself
a pity party!

I know! I'm just as surprised
as you are.

This year alone,
for y'boy rome,
has just been
absolutely,
completely,
horrendously,
all around
utterly FUBAR.

Oh, but . . .
guess what else!?

You're ALL invited!

I know! I'm so miserably
fuckin' UNexcited.

I'm thinkin'
deflated balloons,
sad-faced cartoons.

Oh!
Oh!
Oh!

The best part . . .
I almost forgot.

You're gonna
absolutely LOVE
this commotion.

'Cause you can even
play Pin the Tail . . .

wait for it

. . . on every single one
of my mixed emotions.

How's that,
for goin' all out . . .
as a show of my
pitiful devotion?

Without YOU,
there is no ME . . .
the foundin' father of

"self-loathin' promotions."

Or,

"tapped, yet unrooted"—for short.

God,
I'm feelin' so
out of sorts.

What the fuck . . .

RIGHT NOW . . .
as you're readin'
your way through
the previous parties
that I've held for myself,
throughout the years,

I'm sittin' here
all alone,
gettin' drunk,
once again,
off a fully-stocked case
of Tears.

I started off,
with Tears Light.

I could (for the most part)
maintain my composure,
on Light Tears.

But fairly recently,
I've become the product
of all of my fears.

Light Tears . . .
they no longer soothe
my confliction.
I've developed a rather
uncommon addiction.

My name is rome,
and I'm a bawl-o-holic.

Yes, I'm addicted to
bawlin' my fuckin' eyes out,
cryin' until the next level
of comfort nears.

At least
until I've reached
an emotional high,
that no longer makes
me feel so low . . .
in the eyes of my peers.

But it appears I've written
my way into a place
where•everyone•knows•my•g'damn•name

Raise a glass, motherfuckers . . .
"Cheers!"

That was our class's graduation song.
Here's to high school glory!

Even better . . .
here's to everyone
that's ever chosen
NOT TO
listen to BOTH sides

of a story . . .

. . . before choosin'
to judge ME accordingly.

"Two-'n-a-half years wasted."
Sounds like a small portion
of my seedhood, reportedly.

Fuck You, BITCH!
Without pullin' out—aborted me.

In front of each 'n
every one of you,
I'm breakin' down
as I rhyme—to cry.

No need to ask yourself,
"Why?"

I'm 'bout to tell you.
Shit . . .
I ain't even gonna mutter
one solitary word
of a lie.

To anyone that asks me
about this particular leaf,
I've begun to say, "They died."

Not in real life.
But the person
I once knew, 'n loved,
in my eyes—they died.

The day they allowed

a leaf to blow in,
'n make up new rules
regardin' visitations
(I should say "lack thereof")
which OUR tree
has been unwillingly forced
to abide.

I tried . . .
I honestly fuckin' tried . . .

but when they were asked
about the situation between us,
to no one's surprise,
they blatantly lied.

Causin' the cracks in that branch
of the tree to completely divide.

THAT's where the state of my
last pity party currently resides.

Sad . . .
like that branch, full of leaves,
as it withers, 'n dies.

pours out cries

Which leads me to a *totally*
different pity party—the one
that continues to burn my insides.

This one's for the GUYS!
(And some of you females,
if the situation applies.)

Yes, a P.S.A. to the fellas.
YOU readin' this—take my **ADVICE**!

Now, listen . . .
if you're faced with the task
of becomin' a single leaf,
in a new relationship,
DO NOT give up
your parental rights.

DO NOT fall captive
to insecure spite.

If not for yourself,
do it for your seeds.

Grow some co—Jones,
some *cojones*,
some stones . . .

a pair of fuckin'
testicles . . .

cabrón!

It's time we take back our frickin' pants
from that (vindictive) significant other,
stand up for them seeds, 'n fight!

The fuck is wrong
with us, man!?

God created **US**
with two legs
'n a fuckin' kickstand!

There's absolutely no excuse
that we should use
for not standin' up
on our OWN
three legs—g'damn . . .

That's the beauty of
bein' a g'damn MAN!

I'm sayin' . . .

it's time **WE** remove
the trainin' wheels
'n begin to advance.

Put back on
our big-boy pants,
'n take a firm
parental stance.

Then hand them back
their prissy li'l attitude,
'n tell them it's time
to fuckin' prance!

FUCK THEM!

And . . .
should they ever decide
to leave your ass—
right there where you
FINALLY took a stand.

I'll be there for you, dawg.
With an ice-cold
Tears Light (Dry)

in hand.

For YOUR pity party!

IT'S THE SEEDS THAT SUFFER

They say that life is
what you make of it . . .
and here I am,
with idle hands,
'n paint all over my face.

Color me imperfect.
Still lookin' for my niche.
Tryin' to find my place . . .

in an inexcusable situation
that's fully shadowed—by disgrace.

I'm not quite sure how
I initially fit in,
but I'm positive that I hate
this bitter taste . . .

left in my mouth,
by all of the lost time,
that we selfishly waste.

Someone's gotta break
this vicious cycle.
We can't keep allowin' it
t'go on—THIS way.

I'm speakin' to ALL of you,

that supported this—idle.
I'm callin' YOU ALL out—today.

Any one of you that ignored it
for your own selfish reasons . . .
YOU SHOULD ALL BE ASHAMED.

Every single one of you
have committed treason!
It's time that each of you
assume your share of the blame.

"Leaves" need to start actin' like leaves.

Our seeds shouldn't have had to suffer
as the direct result of
hurt feelings—or OUR dismay.

Our seeds need t'be allowed to act as seeds!

To interact,
run around,
laugh,
'n play . . .

TOGETHER

From any of us—
they NEVER should've been taken away.

It's been years since relationships were banished.
Time's flown by—so fast . . .

I know that it appears that we just vanished.
It hurts knowin' that we can't get back
any of the time—that's passed.

TAPPED YET UNROOTED

Sometimes leaves make decisions
that (at the time) are profoundly rash.

And put what's best for the seeds
predominantly last.

Unfortunately, now they're bein' raised
similarly to OUR past.

Separated from one another.
None of us ever wanted that.

We just always hoped for so much more
for them 'n their upbringin'
than we'd ever had
(. . . and, in some ways, they already have.)

I've stayed up late, many nights—hurtin' bad.
Just thinkin' about them—feelin' sad.

None of our seeds deserved
any of this (not a tad).
It's not at all their fault
that our tradition's outlandishly mad.

To each 'n every one of them . . .
so many apologies need t'be made.

To **OUR** seeds:

As the oldest seed in this situation,
I feel obligated to start the brigade.

I've always tried to lead
what I've deemed
an honest existence.

To attack every aspect of life
with integrity 'n persistence.

But there have been certain challenges,
within our family structure,
that I've met with the utmost resistance.
And, for that, I'M TRULY SORRY.

There have been many
days that have turnt into nights,
where I've failed t'be able
to tell all of our seeds, "I love you!"

And that, although we can't always be together,
"I'd never place anythin' above you."

You should always know, 'n be told . . .
that we ALL love you.
And, for that, I'M ALSO SORRY!

Unfortunately, right now,
our hands are tied
by pre-existing family rules—
we've ALL felt forced to abide.

If you've been told anythin' different . . .
I'm here to tell you that somebody's lied.

We've made every attempt
to keep the peace.
Believe me when I say that
WE'VE TRIED.
And we've ALL FAILED . . .
miserably . . . by 'n by.

For that, I'M EXTREMELY SORRY!

All that I can really hope for
is that you learn from our mistakes.
And that you do whatever it takes,
to (someday) reconnect—with one another.

And when you do,
please be kind to each other.
I'd love for all of you to have
the types of positive relationships,
that we as "leaves" are currently
missin' out on with one another.

I guess I hope that you all
find a way to start fresh.

Never, EVER, look back,
or repeat our pettiness.

You'll save yourselves chapters of stress.
Love others, the way you want t'be loved,
'n don't you ever settle for anythin' less . . .

I promise you'll be happier humans
because of it.

I love you ALL!

SADNESS IS

Sadness is . . .
the tinglin' sensation
in my forehead.
The subtle shakin'
of my brow.

The wellin' up
beneath my eyelids.
The struggle to fight back
liquid emotions
the best that I know how.

Sadness is . . .
blurred vision.
In every sense of those
unforeseen words.

Sadness is . . .
each cry for help
that's ever gone unheard.

Sadness is . . .
the tear drops,
on a cellular screen,
brought upon by
the writin' of the poem
at hand.

While tryin' to cope
with the larger scope
of underlyin' problems
that you'll never fully
understand . . .

Sadness is . . .
pushin' through each day,
with the anticipation
of (the inevitable) bad news.

I'm forever thinkin'
that they'll pass away,
in a deep, dark sleep,

from the various medications,
that they have a tendency
to overly abuse.

There's only so many times
that one can use
that same old
inexcusable excuse.

"I forgot what I had taken.
So, two or more pills,
I've accidentally misused."

Sadness is . . .
the helpless feelin'
of concern for their well bein',
since bein' well . . .
they've obviously refused.

Fuck it . . . let's flip a coin.
Heads or tails?
Either way—every last one of us
is eventually goin' to lose.

Sadness is . . .
all of the obvious indications
that no one makes it out
ALIVE.

And they may die,
ahead of their time,
in an out-of-control,
spiralin', downward
nose dive.

Sadness is . . .

that guilty feelin',
in the pit
of my stomach.

As I stand by—helplessly,
watchin' them plummet
from the tip
of their summit.

They're livin' the HIGH life,
while extractin' new lows
(even for them)
from it.

No matter what
I say or do,
it seems too late
for them
to overcome it.

Sadness is . . .
spoken word
through a silent pen.

A "forget-me-not"
written as a means
to an end.

Know that
I'll always love you.

Never goodbye . . .

until I see you.
See you, again.

SWEDISH BOY

I once used the term
"deLEAFed."

I literally put the
LEAF in deed.

'Cause no matter
what happens in my life,
they'll always be my
LEAF—indeed.

I've never been
that type of boy.

I had too much
testosterone-based
male pride.

I've never told them
how I truly feel.

I didn't wanna
make them sad . . .
I never wanted
to see them cry.

I've never said
goodbye to them.

To me,
that just doesn't
feel at all right.

"I'll talk to you later, now . . ."
is how I'd normally
say good night.

I've taken life
for granted, now . . .
not just yours,
but also mine.

"Later" almost didn't
come for me, now . . .
'n I wished
I'd said goodbye.

And that I love you, now.
With all of this
broken heart,
that I often feel
misbeatin'—on the inside.

I promise I'll do better, now.
I'll try my best,
to make things right.

Tomorrow may not come,
for me, now.

So,
today is my "good night" . . .

Now,
what I couldn't say in person,
I knew that I could always write.

But I didn't want my words
to ever come off as

rude, or impolite.

No matter how hard I've tried . . .
you 'n I never became
all that tight.

A lot of that had t'do with others.

I'd like to say that
I'm okay with it . . .
but that statement wouldn't
be accurate—nor right.

It really sucks that you always felt
like you had to choose a side
of an imaginary, drawn-out line.

And not because the side you chose
usually wasn't mine . . .

but more towards the fact
that you were placed
in that position.

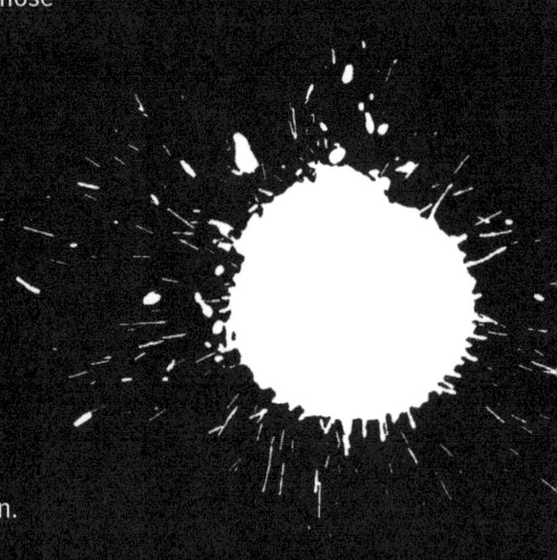

I never wanted t'be
your opposition.

I guess that feelin' like
an unwanted acquisition
set me up for that predisposition.
I never had any other choice.

My actions have always
been my voice . . .
'n lately, I've purposely
been distant.

I haven't made any efforts,
long distance.
As I've been keepin' to myself,
with sheer consistence,

'n you appear to have done the same.

I just want you to know
that I don't hold you to blame.

You've always felt like
others couldn't do without you,
'n I could take care of myself . . .
as you'd, so often, claim.

And fairly recent,
I've been startin' to feel the same.

I've exhausted my brain,
listenin' to the same ol' same.
I have to accept the fact
that this will never change.

And I believe in my heart
that I finally have . . .
'n it feels so strange . . .
knowin' that we've
become somewhat estranged . . .

but in this thought,
I still find comfort
'n joy . . .

'cause no matter
what happens in our lives,
I'll always be a proud

Svensk pojke.

Jag älskar dig!

GET THE HINT

Some of my relationships
have burnt out.
While others slowly fizzle.

The list of people
whom I trust
continues to dwindle.

When each of the fires
are done burnin',
there will be nothin' left
to rekindle.

My days of repairin' burnt bridges
just went up in smoke.
There's no fixin' relationships
that were manufactured
of swindle.

With everythin' that
I've ever told them,
they saw as an opportunity
to steal some of the spotlight.

If I told them I was workin'
on a female friend's website,
they'd say that I was
"workin' on another man's wife."

If I told them that I talked
to a female, for a while,
about our kids,
they'd say that I "scared her,"
'n she now thinks that I'm a stalker,
"so, don't anyone tell rome
where she lives!"

I'd say that I can't believe it.
What kind of a relative says
such outlandish shit?

Then I remember 'bout whom
I'm speakin',
'n the reality cuts deep,
down within.

Yet, they still wonder
why I share nothin',
that's personal
with this kin.

They don't fully comprehend . . .
that it's a truly
fucked-up world
that we live in . . .

when I've gotta watch
everythin' I say,
every fuckin' day,
around the supposedly
closest members of
ancestral skin.

Maybe this time

the reality will finally start
to kick in.

ANSWER ME

The Good Lord works
in a mysterious way.

I know that He couldn't possibly
grant us every single miracle
for which we pray.

I remember wakin' up,
feelin' sad as hell,
that next day.

Another prayer unanswered.

The night before,
he took his final breath.
I said, "Goodbye, Gramps,"
'n watched his death.

FUCK CANCER!

Neuroblastoma has invaded
the happy home
of one of the bravest seeds
that I've ever known.

Although he's not mine.
I still love him,
like each of my own.

Continue to battle,
with the courage
'n overwhelmin' strength
that you've always shown.

While he fights
the battle of his life,
his parents remain hopeful,
as they continuously pray
for their answer.

B. STRONG—"To remission, 'n beyond."

FUCK CANCER!

I know you fought
until the end.
Because I've NEVER seen
you quit, my friend.

One of the strongest *brothers*
that I've ever had.
Gone too soon.
This hurts, so bad . . .

I think about you every day.
It sucks.

I hate that you 'n I'd lost touch.

I regret that I waited
'til it was too late.

I should have stepped up
to the plate,
'n taken the time

to communicate.

There are so many questions,
that I wish you were still here
to answer.

I love 'n miss you, Opie.
Rest in peace.

FUCK CANCER!

I think an awful lot—about the past.
I think even more—about the present . . .
now, please listen. *(Por favor, escucha.)*

One of my favorite poets once said,
" . . . the truth is, there's no hope for the future."

But givin' up hope . . .

givin' up . . .
it's just not somethin'
that I could see myself
ever get used ta'.

I believe that miracles occur
each 'n every day.

I believe in the motto
"where there's a will,
there's always a way."

I believe that there's
someone listenin',
every time we pray.

I believe in my heart
that a cure will be found
one blessed day.

But as for today . . .
my family finds itself
once again prayin'
for another miracle,
in the form of a
positive answer.

Somethin's got to give.
WHAT THE FUCK, CANCER?!

FORGET ME NOT

When my seeds are self-efficient
and they're all fully grown . . .

When they've become young adults,
and have lives of their own . . .

When they, someday, become fathers,
and start showin' their kids everythin'
that they've been shown . . .

When they're instillin' the same morals, 'n values,
that I would (more than) happily condone . . .

I just want t'be remembered.
I'd really like t'be remembered.

When I've become the elderly gentleman,
that I once only dreamed that I could be . . .

TAPPED YET UNROOTED

When I've accomplished everythin'
on that ever-so-lengthy bucket list . . .

When they're lookin' through old pictures,
'n stumble upon some that include me . . .

When they're all together,
speakin' of all the good times that they miss . . .

I just want t'be remembered.
I'd really like t'be remembered.

When life turns cold,
cause we've grown old . . .

When my will to live,
has been held at bay . . .

When I forget everythin'
that I've ever been told . . .

When I'm at a loss,
for poetic words to place on display . . .

I just want t'be remembered.
I'd really like t'be remembered.

When all is said 'n done
and I've seen my last day . . .

When daylight turns to dusk,
and my blue skies fade to gray . . .

When my candle has burnt out—at both ends
and I've worn out my stay . . .

When I close my eyes that one last time,
and I drift, then pass, away . . .

I just want t'be remembered.
I'd really like t'be remembered.

When my words no longer leave my mouth,
but still speak clairvoyantly—on paper . . .

When my presence is no longer visual,
but my soul lives on—in spiritual vapor . . .

When they quote from famous poets
that wrote of love, life, family, scandals,
'n miscellaneous capers . . .

When I've long gone home to Heaven,
and I'm restin' peacefully beside my makers . . .

I just want t'be remembered.
I'd really like t'be remembered.

GOOD VS. EVIL

I have a way with words.
I've a mean streak inside.

I'm a voice with many followers,
'n there's nothin' left
for me to hide.

But which do I listen to?
The angel to the left,
or the devil to the right?

POETIC WORD SLAUGHTER

The angelic side of me's
tellin' me to stop.
The devilish side of me's
screamin' at the top of his lungs,
"JUST FUCKIN' WRITE!"

Normally, for me,
this is a no-brainer.
But I just cannot,
mentally,
pick a side.

I'm fightin' through this pain.
They've scattered throughout
my brain.

On one hand,
I should forgive, 'n forget.
On the other hand,
I show so much
fuckin' disdain.

I wanna ball it into a fist,
'n release a factual fury
of blame.

Look what you've made me do!
Look what I've done
with the shame,
the hurt,
the mud . . .
through which you continually
drag my name.

I'm publicly demolishin' my closet.
Clearin' out space

for you to hang . . .
out with every coward,
that turns their backs
on the roots,
from whence they claimed
their friggin' name.

Fuck an apology.
Fuck workin' shit out.
Fuck!
Things between us
won't EVER . . .
'n I mean NEVER . . .
be any fraction
of the same.

& & & & AND . . .
fuck anyone that
strongholds my reputation.
You'll never be ME.
That shit's pathetically lame.

I'll say it, 'til I'm blue in the face.
Fuck all of those childish games,
to which our tree
claims their fame.

HEART TO HEART

I cried,
on my way
in to work.

You're not gone.

But the thought
of it—hurts.

I refuse to
come to terms,
with the worst.

I'm prayin' that
their diagnosis
gets reversed.

Last night . . .
you kicked my hand,
for the first time,
'n I thought to myself,
"I don't want this moment
with you—t'be our last."

I'm not afraid to admit
that I've already grown
attached.

This is all happenin'
so fast.

I have no idea
how in the hell
we're gonna cope,
if the Lord chooses
for you to pass.

I honestly don't.

The doctors have all
but written you off.
Yet your mommy 'n I,

we still have hope . . .

that a lot of love,
'n daily prayer,
will be your antidote.

Although, we both know
that it's gonna take
so much more.

You've got a rough
road ahead you . . .
a tough fight
still in store.

I just pray that
it isn't much more
than your tiny body
can withstand or endure.

That this "trisomy"
is no longer a factor,
'n your heart's irregularities
will be fully cured.

This is one of those topics
that Daddy doesn't
discuss with your mommy,
for her own good.

Stress isn't good
for her (or you)
right now,
'n she's goin' through
so much more,
than I believe

any woman ever should . . .

‘n I made a promise to myself,
that I’d protect her,
(both physically ‘n emotionally)
the very best that I could.

‘Cause I know that,
without a doubt,
if your mommy had the chance
t’do that for us,
in a heartbeat she would.

But I won’t lie to you, buddy.
Right now,
I’m really scared.

Your mommy’s been so brave,
but she’s really not prepared.
Nor am I . . .

nor will we ever pretend t’be.

You’re not even here, yet.
And you mean so much
to your mommy ‘n me.

To think that this thought started
with you kickin’ my hand,
through your mommy’s belly,
last night . . .

Please, my baby boy.
Please continue to fight,
with all of your might.

Just like your daddy did.

;

Semicolon.
Heart's semi-swollen.
Thoughts heavy rollin'.
Blood steady strollin'.
There's no controllin' . . .

these suicidal **TENDENCIES**.
Constantly feelin' the weight of
TEN DENSE SEAS.

And I'm drownin'.

Yeah,
y'boy's been battlin' demons,
since the tender age of nine.

Yes,
it's been the same amount of time,
since I've been sayin' that "I'm fine."

Yet,
there's been at least a time,
or three,
where they've gotten the best o' me,
'n I tripped o'er that "fine line."

Okay,
I threw myself across it.
With tears tricklin' out m'faucet.
Unfortunately, there's no off-set.

TAPPED YET UNROOTED

Each failed attempt to pause it
has me cleanin' out my closet.

And I'm drownin'.

Beneath this mass of memories.
Bequeath these massive reveries . . .
guess this is all that's left o' me.
These tears shed to the left o' me.

As I sit here, 'n hesitantly ponder,
m'mind starts to resistantly wander.
Absence has never helped me grow any fonder
of this depression that drags me down yonder.

For years I've been treadin' lightly.
All my fears I've been deadin' slightly.
One by one, overcomin' 'em nightly.
Graspin' for droplets o' sanity tightly.

And I'm drownin'.

Trapped in this storm of sunder.
Day by day, I slip a li'l further under.
Anxiety 'n depression—my lightnin' 'n thunder.
With tears rainin' down my face, in a blunder . . .

"WHEN WILL MY MISERY END!?"
I constantly wonder.

Always so fuckin' depressed.
This weighted burden lays across my chest.
On the inside I'm a g'damn mess.
But . . . on the outside . . .

I'm clean-cut, got my shit together,

'n I'm always neatly dressed.

And I'm drownin'.

I jus' wanted you to know,
that you're not alone!
Because I'm with you . . .
—rome

";"

OFF MY "CHESS"

If my life had a theme song,
I wonder what it'd be . . .

I've cried so many nights,
'n dreamt so many (unwanted) dreams.

I've awoken, scared to death,
from my own loud, petrified screams.

What do they gain, at my expense?
What is it, from me, that they all need?

What is the reason for my existence?
Who am I supposed t'be?

I know I've got a greater purpose,
hidden somewhere, deep, inside of me.

I've tried to drag it out.
I've tried to intervene.

I've tried carvin' my own niche.
But my pieces never seem to fit.

God, what am I supposed t'do here?
Why should I continue human bein'?

It would be easier to rid myself—from all this shit.
Why am "I" not allowed to quit?

When do you determine who has it too rough?
When do you determine that a life is too tough?
When do you determine that "enough is enough"?

My thoughts are cavin' in.
These walls are paper thin.
I'm foldin' under the pressure—from within.
Can we start all over again?
Where should we begin?

If I thought I had all the answers,
under these circumstances,
I'd never turn to you.

I'm still learnin' from my mistakes,
'n I've been known to make a few.

You've offered me life without direction(s).
In return I've chosen paths
without clear views.

I don't feel like they're at all justified
with all that I'm forced to prove.

Life's not about win or lose.
There's never been an option to choose.

Out of all of the pieces on the board,
I'm the ONE they most commonly abuse.

I'm just a pawn, in the games
that they play.
It seems I'm runnin' out of moves.

Yet, you've taken every step beside me,
as I'm still tryin' to fill my own shoes.

I couldn't do this without you.
You've always selflessly helped me through.

If I haven't said it enough . . .
thank you!

From the bottom of my heart,
I thank you . . .

but, before I forget to ask—

Lord, please tell me . . .
what should I do?

Life's gotten so hard.

WET PAPER BAGS

You should always be mindful,
towards what you say—near li'l ears.
Those words always make their way back.

They've told us about the
hateful things you had to say.

You've shown a blatant disregard for tact.

I can think of several mature ways
to properly deal with this mess.

Straightforward, 'n to the point?
Yeah, that works best—I guess.

So, I'ma be blatantly honest.
Nothin' said in jest . . .

Since one's been fillin' ears,
on some ridiculousness,
the other felt it their right
to come ridicule us next.

Which is where most
of the current/past
pettiness manifests.

Now we've gotta deal
with these two fuckin' assholes,
barkin' untruthfully, from the chest.

M'bad . . . I should say that one's a clone,
who's formed an opinion of their own.
Not by the actions that I've shown,
but by their ill feelings that've grown.
They've got me most commonly known
(to the seeds) as a "bad influence."

They never should have brought
any of ours into this.

Let alone tell them,
"You seeds don't know,

who rome really is."

The other tells them,
"He's not as tough
as you think he is.
I use to beat him up
(all the time), before
phones took quick vids."

Got me R•O•T•F•Laughin'.
I can't believe this shizz.

You can ask anyone who knows,
who's REALLY given who the biz . . .

I can promise you that **THEY** know
that I've never EVER lost a fight.

And I'm the exact opposite of who
you tell them I am, out of sheer spite.
Y'all must be fuckin' jokin'—right!?

Seriously.
That shit will NEVER happen.

SECOND GUESSIN'

I've been writin' in my feelings.
Not showin' any sort of remorse.

My pen's been steady healin'.
This time I've let nature—run its course.

As promised, in the beginning, while coerced.

There's jus' so much—that needed t'be said.
Which has reduced me—to this final resort . . .

This was t'be . . . **IT**.
The ULTIMATE—retort.

[thinkin' back]

Bite marks—on my tongue
Permanently indented . . .

All the shit I never said, back then . . .
fuck—I would've meant it.

I always wondered if those words
would've reached the ears
for which—they were intended.

I couldn't have made that shit up.
Those truths—were not invented.

But . . .
because I chose to sit—'n stew . . .
in a Crock-Pot that reeked of brews,
my mind's, now, full-on fermented . . .

I stressed myself—the hell out,
'n caused myself to become
fuckin' demented.

Now dementia's settled in,
like the space—in my mind
that they've all but fuckin' rented.

[**I TRIED TO SPEAK UP**—sooner.]

Instead . . .
this book is how I've FINALLY vented.

I'd written a lot of fucked-up shit.
And—at the time—I know I meant it.

Anger had me so caught up, in my feelings,
'n I lashed out, at those—that sent it.

On some levels—I was wrong.
I think I knew it—all along.

But I was speakin' so much truth . . .
that I jus' let loose—'n carried on.

I knew I had to let it out . . .
'n to all that anger say,
"So long!"

Then I went back through this book TWICE,
rewrote, 'n removed, a lot of their wrong.

Now I'm back to poundin' right along,
to the heartbeat—of my own "GONG!"

As if those were the lyrics—to my swan song.
Thousands of words—I couldn't honorably prolong.

And I'm STILL not even sure they'll get it.
They never frickin' get it.

Our past was so fragmented.
But in my mind, the memories cemented.

I'm sorry I chipped away.

But I'm not sorry—they slipped away.
I've said what I had to say.

The past is the past.
I'm movin' forward.
Not lookin' back . . .
'n THAT'S all I gotta say—about that!

THOSE WORDS

HE IS SOMEBODY . . .
the who
usually doesn't matter . . .

HE IS THE ONE . . .
the cause
of all of their ludicrous chatter . . .

HE IS A LIFE . . .
whose feelings
they repetitively shatter . . .

HE IS AN OPEN BOOK . . .
his past
is a popular chapter . . .

HE IS PROOF . . .
that attention
is what they've always been after.

HE IS TARGETED . . .
by allegations
for which they use his back for.

HE IS ALONE . . .
in struggles
without a sole benefactor . . .

HE IS INTERNALLY BROKEN . . .
slow-healin'
is his mentality fracture.

HE IS MOVIN' ON . . .
in search
of a greener pasture.

HE IS BETTER OFF . . .
orphaned
from here on out, that is his stature.

"You should have been adopted!"

REST IN PEACE, BABY BOY

10/11/15 11:44 A.M. — 10/11/15 6:44 P.M.

Today you came into this world,
'n flipped ours upside down.
Mommy 'n Daddy were so very scared
as she changed into her surgical gown.
Quickly preparin' Mommy for surgery
(an emergency C-section),
doctors 'n nurses are rushin' all around.
You're several weeks too early.
So, comfort (in this moment) can't be found.

Waitin' impatiently behind that curtain;
she announced,

"Baby's out!"
But you didn't make any sounds.
Organized chaos floods the room.
My mind is so consumed . . .
["Healthy," Trisomy 18, or Downs?]

A single tear rolled down Mommy's face.
I use my finger—to wipe it away.
We haven't given up faith.
Yet, there's a distinct feelin'
that you're homeward bound.

A door opens to the left.
The doctor's words cut through my chest.
"DO YOU WANT US TO CONTINUE?"
We say, "YES."
We still have hope, more or less.
A gentleman in the room's reassured us
that they're doin' their very best.
Again the door opens—to the left.
This time I nod.
The answer's still "YES."

Until he takes his final breath,
we've chosen not to concede death.
We love you too much,
not to try.

We'd have given anything,
just to hear you cry.

But we'd have to settle,
for an open eye.

Sometimes a life,
isn't meant t'be.

This is so difficult,
for your mommy ‘n me.

We said a prayer to God,
‘n set you free.

Mommy held you,
until you passed.

We kissed you, farewell.
God, this all happened so fast.

There’s no words to express
the emptiness we all feel.

We fully believe that
God needed another angel.

It just doesn’t seem real.

Rest in peace, Baby Boy.
We love you!

Always ‘n forever . . .
Mommy ‘n Daddy.

FAVORITISM, NOW!?

It’s the mornin’ after
our angel was born.

It was an extremely
difficult first night,
as we’d just begun

to mourn.

I've gotta finally break
the heart-wrenchin' news
to all of my family,
'n I'm still feelin' torn.

Less than twenty-four hours
since our baby boy
passed away.

I know I've got to
share my secret.
But I'm not ready.

Not today . . .

I'd kept his medical issues
to myself—seven months
of absolute silence.

Out of fear that "someone"
would say somethin' disrespectful,
'n I'd resort—to violence.

So much stress to deal with,
'n it's hit me—all at once.

Knowin' their track records
for talkin' all kinds of shit,
I felt the need to
beat 'em—to the punch.

Which is why I decided
not to tell them at all.
Not a single one,

in the entire spoiled bunch.

Sure, I confided in a sibling.
And a close-knit group
of friends.

But I kept it from them.
And anyone else
that I'd felt wouldn't
be able to comprehend . . .
that this was a sensitive subject,
once again . . .

a delicate piece of information,
regardin' my unborn
(now deceased)
son's health,
that I chose to defend,
'til the bitter end.

And by me makin' one
(ONE) single phone call,
I was immediately reminded
why our family structure
is so unappealin' . . .

"Who's gonna tell SO 'n SO?"
"Can I tell SO 'n SO?"
"SO 'n SO should know."
"Can I tell SO 'n SO, now?"
"What if SO 'n SO finds out, 'n I didn't tell THEM?"
"What about SO 'n SO's feelings?"

What about SO 'n SO's feelings . . .

SO 'n SO's FEELINGS!?

Yep, this is the
exact type of shit
with which I'm (already)
currently dealin'.

My son passed away,
'n this one's overly worried
about SO 'n SO feelings.

I just told you
the absolute worst news
of my entire life.

I haven't even BEGUN
to think about
my heart healin'.

And your concern
has already shifted
away from my son's death . . .

then you question the reason
why I didn't tell you, sooner.
But you're strugglin' to keep
THIS piece of information
under your breath?

This shit doesn't make
any kind of sense.

And a few days later,
when the arrangements were set
to lay him down for eternal rest . . .

"Can SO 'n SO go to the services?"
"SO 'n SO should really be there."

"Do you want me to tell SO 'n SO it's okay?"
"Have you changed your mind about SO 'n SO?"
"Can SO 'n SO go?"
"Is it alright, if SO 'n SO just pays THEIR respects?"

What the hell else should I expect . . .
I mean, what the FUCK . . . really!?

How do I not dwell,
when they're always
in my g'damn head, non-ideally?

Mornin', noon, 'n night.
Car ride, at work, in bed.
I can't catch a fuckin' break.
Over the years I've often
wished that it was me
that was taken—instead.

Someone developed this
type of pyramid scheme,
in which I fall at the bottom
of the tree hierarchy.

"We know that we don't
have to worry about you.
You've always taken care
of yourself."

What a bunch of
horseshit malarkey.

Now, I'm not talkin' any trash.
Or actin' at all snarky.

The worst tragedy

of my life just occurred,
'n they've got me
fieldin' ridiculous questions.

How do I "respectfully" say,
"FUCK OFF, MOTHERFUCKER"!?

I'm open to all suggestions.

Don't get me wrong.
I love them all . . . I really do.
I'm just so frickin' tired,
of their off-base projections.

I could write an entire
fuckin' book,
based solely upon
all of my fucked-up
recollections.

Oh, wait . . .

Anyways,
at an early age
I came to terms
with the fact that
I've never been
the tree's top selection.

(Which is probably why
I no longer fear rejection.)

But dealin' with the same bullshit
over, 'n over, 'n over again
has become as unpleasantly
uncomfortable as

tryin' to stand up to piss . . .
at three o'clock in the mornin',
inside of the toilet bowl,
through a (fully functionin')
penile erection.

I'm on a porcelain downward spiral.

I think it's time
for me 'n mine
to change the course
of our direction.

It's time to drop some peeps
from my extensive collection.

dial tone
"Umm, hello!?"

M'bad!
I must've lost 'em . . .
yeah, that's it,
"bad connection."

REPEAT OFFENDER

I'm on the
social network,
occupyin' my mind,
while sadly reminiscin'.

When an article
in my news feed
shines out—off of the page . . .

as if to, brightly, glisten.

It appears as though
my earlier prediction,
has tragically come
to fruition.

I tried to forewarn them,
to watch that monster
around those frickin' seeds.
Call it parental intuition.
(It was common sense.)

But, just like those
previous incidents,
when we were
all small seeds . . .
they refused to listen.

God, I wish
I'd have finished him
off back then . . .

When I was
first thrown
in that fucked-up
position.

But that opportunity
was lost.
It's gone.
Regretfully missin'.

What a fucked-up tree
for anyone to choose
to raise up kids in.

shakin' my head

disbelief

full body sadness

Right now I'm
really feelin' like
I could fuckin' bite
the shit out of
the ass end of
that rotten frickin' apple . . .

all the way to
the putrid core
that lies within.

Exposin' unpleasant
amounts of memory-
induced sin—on him!

I'm not talkin'
Adam 'n Eve.

I'm talkin' 'bout
tearin' shit up,
ONE LAST TIME,
'til the fisticuffs fin.

I don't consider them
my fuckin' family.

It's a g'damn shame
what they've done
to unsuspectin' kin.
Not to mention the

unspeakable that
they'd already done
to MYSELF 'n them.

Go ahead 'n
gather up all of those
ignorant-ass members,
'n their fucked-up friends.

For old times' sake,
they can watch us
take another quick spin
around that small
living room den.

Real talk.
No pen.

Let 'em huddle
back around us
in that squared circle,
like they used t'do
when we were
mere chil•dren.

One last human
cockfight . . .

Just the two of us . . .
in the middle of those
sick cocksuckers,
all over again.

Only this time
we can handle
THIS SHIT

like grown fuckin' men.

That means there
won't be any of that
grabbin' my balls . . .
like a bitch-ass hen.

We can solve this,
ONCE 'n FOR ALL.

So that you'll never
be able to offend
another individual
again!

SILENT CONFUSION

Our long ride home
from Hartford Hospital
was understandably quiet.

Barely did we speak.

I'm usually good with words.
What a time (for me)
t'go unusually meek.

As I watched pain,
after anguish,
flow steadily down
both of her cheeks . . .
'til halfway through our travels
when, silently, she falls into
a much-needed sleep.

By now, you all know that
I'm no stranger to pain.

But our son's death
has cut me so deep.

All alone with my thoughts,
back into my head—I slowly creep . . .
towards two of the many phone calls
that I'd received—while my eyes
welled up 'n leaked.

One I could tell was sincere,
while the other sounded rather sleek.

I haven't heard from either of you,
in well over fifty-two g'damn weeks!

Oh, NOW you wanna share my pain?
Well, aren't you just frickin' sweet.

You could have called,
back when times were good!

Instead you waited,
'til I'm down 'n out . . .
'n feelin' weak.

I've always tried t'be so strong.
And, right now, that's what
she needs me t'be.

No one expects me to crumble.
But they know that I'ma crack,
when I finally break down

‘n weep.

‘N NOW they wanna share my pain . . .
like I’ma pull ‘em up a fuckin’ seat!?

“Yeah, this would be
the perfect time
to have ourselves
an extensive conversation
‘bout what you can do for me.”

NOT!

Right now,
I don’t know what to think,
let alone—believe.

All I wanna do . . .
all I really wanna do,
is grieve.

Please . . .

if you have a heart . . .
any kind of a heart . . .
let me grieve—in peace.

God,
I can’t believe
my baby boy
was taken away—deceased.

tears* *tears* *tears* *tears

RAINY DAYS

God . . .

It never gets easy.
Sayin' "goodbye."

Some may handle it with grace . . .
but, I've never been that guy.

A kiss upon the cheek,
with tear-filled eyes.

A smile from the doorway.
He was always overflowin'—with such pride.

Now each song on the radio,
makes me wanna break down—'n cry.

Another dreaded Sunday . . .
'n I'm not ready—for the ride.

I'll think of you every day, Moose . . .
when I look up towards the sky.

As of right now, the sun is faintly shinin'.
Yet, you also (downward) cry.

Teardrops fallin' upon me,
from a semi-clouded sky.

You've joined a class of angels.
Granted your wings . . .
learnin' how to fly.

There's a sudden chill—that fills the air.
I've a touch of glossy eyes.

This task is, overly, unsettlin'.
I'm havin' an extremely difficult time.

I just don't have it in me . . .
to tell you goodbye.

I can't say that word.
In fact, I've an unwillingness—to try.

'Cause I know we'll meet again.
When the time that comes—is mine.

And I've forced myself to believe,
that you're takin' care of our baby boy.
As you wait, for us—on the other side.

You see . . .

I've always had this belief . . .
that tears fall from Heaven,
from those that have died.

To serve as a reminder,
that it IS OKAY for us—to, openly, cry.

When a loved one passes on . . .
it's a heartbreakin', emotional
roller-coaster-of-feelings type of ride.

Here I write to you,
full-on exposin' those feelings.
As I need this pain to, completely, subside.

I understand—in God's hands, we all reside.

. . . Everythin' happens, for a reason.
. . . When it's our time—IT'S OUR TIME.

So, let's take a brief moment,
to think of all of our angels.
On their heavenly journeys—towards the sky.

'N cherish all of the wonderful memories,
as irreplaceable gifts . . .
that they've left us, graciously, behind.

Godspeed,

E.M. Jr. 'n E.C.E

HERE IT IS

Contrary to popular belief,
I was never her favorite—AT ALL . . .

she only kept me close
because she was afraid
that I'd spill everythin' to y'all.

The truth is that
she was a g'damn screwball,
that went as far as to threaten me,
inside of a bathroom stall.

"If you ever tell anyone,
I'll make it hell—FOR YOU ALL!"

. . . And I believed her.

'Cause when crazy tells you, "Don't say shit,"
that's a great indication of your eminent downfall.

Just the visual of her "cat 'o nine tails"
made that an easy one—to call.

You see . . .
I'd gone to the Boogie Ma'am,
'n told her—about my "assault."

But she got extremely angry—with me
'n insisted that
it was all **MY** fault.

"You must've wanted it—
if you placed yourself in that position."

So confused . . .
I'm just a seed!
NEVER, EVER would I have given
ANYONE that type of permission.

Let alone someone of their
pedophilic volition.
Yet, just when you think
you've got all that you need,
in form of pertinent ammunition . . .
you're disarmed.
By an adult, with an even worse predisposition,
than a fuckin' pedophile
on an incestuous mission.

A seed's worst nightmare,
brought to day-lit fruition.

TAPPED YET UNROOTED

Time, 'n time again . . . bet.

It was right after that
that I did what I do best
whenever I'm totally upset.

Here it is:
I forced myself—to forget.

Which I'd later regret . . .
knowin' what I'm 'bout to share.

It's time, my soul, I bare.
This shit's **F.U.B.A.R.**—past repair.

Fucked **U**p **B**eyond **A**ll **R**ecognition?

No, worse . . .

Fucked **U**p **B**eyond **A**ll **R**ome-has-written!

I told you that somewhere
within this outpourin',
I'd conquer all of my fears.

This one's always been my biggest . . .

the risk of feelin' vulnerable,
in front of you—my peers.

After this thought,
my closet's completely empty.
Not a single fuckin'
family-related skeleton
remains forgotten—in there.

Inappropriately touched
by someone I trust.

I've been to Hell,
then back,
then Hell again . . .
without any form of justification.

The "struggle's been so real"
for this "strugglin' with reality" Caucasian.

Didn't get bum-rushed,
but he felt on my nuts . . .
on more than one
uncomfortable occasion.

This time, I opened my eyes—to an odd touch.
His fuckin' mouth—it's near my nuts.
He's all puckered up—no ejaculation.

For years, I've protected my ass—no exaggeration.
I would not "get got"—no penetration.

I've fought so g'damn hard—for self-preservation.
In a fight for your "life," can't be no hesitation.

Thinkin' back, I still can't understand why she refused
to acknowledge this molestation?

The way he openly grabbed my genitals,
in front of everyone
who antagonized our "human cockfight,"
was eerily brazen.

Yes, I'm openly admittin' that
I'm a victim of sexual assault . . .

that stemmed from a beyond-
fucked-up situation—involvin' seed-hazin'.

The reocurrin' stress has
got me feelin' all alone,
even though everybody's home.

I'm keepin' my back pressed firmly
against every fuckin' wall.

Fast forward through all of these years,
'n I'm still panicked with (anxiety-filled) fears,
just walkin' through the g'damn mall.

Out of fear that someone might
cuff the back of my head . . .
or cop a quick feel—of my balls.

PTSD . . .
every friggin' insecurity . . .
memories of abuse . . .
you name it—I've got 'em all.

Every fuckin' one . . .
surprise! Your boy rome is human,
'n right now my eyes are full-on cryin',
while the rest of me is steady fumin'.

I've kept this secret
to myself EVERY day, shit.

But, NO MORE!
FUCK ALL THAT DISMAY SHIT!

I've somethin' that I need to say, shit.
As I'm emptyin' my heart

over some incestuously gay shit.
They knew he was a predator,
but they ain't neva say shit.
Then they threaten to sue me,
over some mentionin'-of-names shit.
If you cannot take any type of
accountability, or responsibility,
that's some really fuckin' lame shit!
This is the LAST g'damn time
I hold my head in shame shit.
I'll no longer place myself to blame shit.
I'ma take out this whole family tree,
frame-by-fuckin'-frame shit.
Until you stop misusin' my g'damn name shit.
It was time t'be more brave shit.
I wasn't takin' this to my grave shit.
I had thoughts to parlay shit.
So I wrote a fuckin' book of the fray shit,
'n put it ALL on display shit.

Fuck it . . . right now,
that's all I've got to say . . . SHIT!

I've lost my seedhood,
my will to live,
'n now my son . . .
what more do I have, for you to take away?

Shit.

SLEEPLESS NIGHT

I try to lead a modest life.
I always practice what I preach.

Every new life lesson,
is another opportunity to teach.
I don't know where we're headed.
The future that we'd planned for you
has now been breached.
Yet there's comfort in just knowin'
that you're with the Lord,
livin' a life of peace.

You see, the world
that we're still livin' in
is far from bein' kind.
We left that hospital
filled of your spirit.
But your tiny li'l body
we were forced to leave—behind.

With that moment, we'll be forever taunted.
As your mommy cried out, emotionally,
". . . But that was the part that I WANTED!"

I understand that we'll all heal
in time.

And I also understand that,
eventually,
Mommy 'n Daddy will be just fine.

But, as for tonight . . .
you're weighin' heavy on my mind.

. . . 'Cause,
right now,
your daddy can't sleep.
As I sit here, in the dark, 'n weep.
You were supposed to come home,

with your mommy 'n me—us three.
Greeted by your sister 'n brothers.
One great, big, happy family.

Your brother points to Mommy's belly
'n proudly yells out, "BABY!"

He doesn't understand that
you've gone to Heaven.
God, this is so unbelievably crazy!

I'm so close to breakin' down.
It could happen so easily.

A lesser me would probably be
on the ground already,
askin' you, "GOD, WHY ME!?"

"WHY HER?"
"WHY HIM?"
"WHY OUR (FAITHFUL) FAMILY?"

Instead, God, I beg for Your forgiveness . . .
from down here—on bended knee.

Although I never gave up faith,
today I questioned YOUR fidelity.

Today, I felt like it was YOU that cheated ME.
But I was wrong.
As a grievin' man, kneelin' before you,
I admit it.
I know right from wrong.
And in my emotional state,
I overdid it.

I've been tryin' t'be so strong,
for so long.
From everyone I know—the pain,
I hid it.

Tonight I'm all done hidin'.
I'm prayin' out loud, 'n such . . .
what I'd give up for you,
to have but one more touch . . .
I'm just missin' our baby boy.
Your mommy 'n daddy miss you so much.

We'll see you on Saturday, my son.
Until then,
I'll do my best—to remain tough.

I love you . . .

CLOSURE

As we stood there,
in the funeral home room,
Mommy 'n I took some time
to quietly let it all soak in.

Our son sits all alone,
on an altar.
His cremated remains restin'
comfortably within
a small, pearl-white, boxed urn,
that's been completely crafted
of a beautiful porcelain.

Atop'd by an angel,

who's consolin' an infant.
Our baby boy is completely
sheltered from sin.

Family 'n friends are now filin' in,
to pay their respects.
They're unaware, as to what to expect.
It's a little before 10 A.M.,
when our son's services are allowed
to begin.

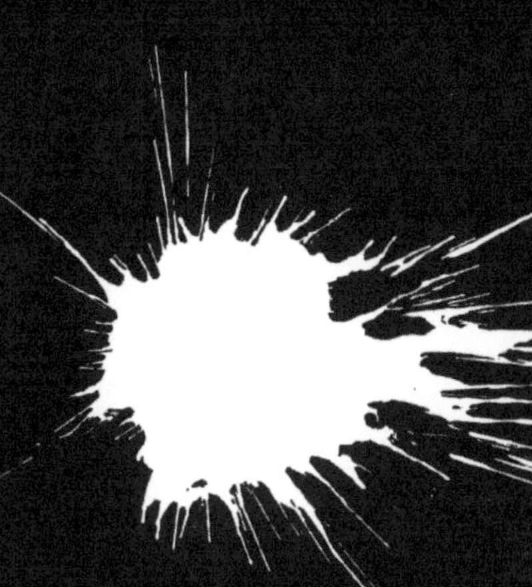

We're without words,
to express how thankful we are,
towards everyone that came
to help us see our baby boy along.

A little ways into the warm embraces,
'n heartfelt condolences,
"Mamina" asks us for our permission,
to sing Baby Boy a Spanish song.

With a beautifully movin' tribute,
soft background chatter turns to silence,
for a brief moment of comfort,
for which many of us had so longed.

". . . There are angels among us."

[Those words couldn't have hit me
as bein' any more true.

Now, I'm a spiritual person . . .
but, if only for a minute,
my train of thought was redirected
towards all of you.

Without the support
that we've received,
for almost a week,
I don't know what my fiancée,
'n I, would do.

The kind words . . .
the acts of generosity . . .
the prayers . . .
the donations . . .
just to name a few.]

Shortly thereafter,
Mommy's Aunty Doll read everyone
her lovingly handwritten poem.
This one part, in particular,
hit me so much harder than I'd shown.

"As we stand here heartbroken,
feelin' so all alone,
the angels are singin' joyously,
'Hallelujah!
Baby Boy has come home.'"

tears

Mommy's cousin R.S.
followed promptly
with a loud bang—upon his drum.
As he emotionally sang his way
through an Indian tribute,
I feel myself start to succumb,
to the sadness that I've felt all along.

After Mommy heads out to check on your brother,
I go to my "safe place" . . .

head down,
eyes closed,
hands coverin' my face.

And I finally allowed myself to cry,
'til I felt their embrace.

Now, I fully understand
that these services are intended
to help give us all some closure.

But I still waited for Mommy to leave,
as not to bring her down (any further)
with my inconsolable exposure.

Which is the reason why I asked them
to please let me know BEFORE she returned,
in order to regain my composure.

. . . And then I apologized to everyone else
in the room.
'Cause it just felt like the right thing t'do.

Mommy returned.
We said our goodbyes.
And we finally left—with you . . .

Our eternal love,
Mommy 'n Daddy.

TAKIN' A STAND

As profound as this may sound . . .
I just wanted you t'be proud.

Damn, that felt so good,
to finally be allowed (by myself)
to say those words—aloud.

Okay,
that's as nice as this will get.

Even if you couldn't hear it.
I know that you're here—in spirit.

Now I've got some shit to say,
'n I'ma fuckin' share it.

Ah, fuck—I jus' cussed.
Screw it . . .
swearin's still a must.
You'll understand—I'm crushed.

I tried to write this before.
But I felt as though I'd rushed.

"When you've been
inappropriately touched
by someone in whom you trust . . ."

You tend to view life—through a different lens.
There's no room, for makin' amends.
Y'all knew this wasn't his first fuckin' offense.
The fuck you mean, "Why am I always so tense"!?
You fucktards should've followed his g'damn trends.
Actin' like you didn't know any of these events.
We were jus' young seeds, livin' a life—of mens.
It's far too late, for any of you LEAVES, to make amends.

Y'know what!?
I really don't give a flyin' fuck who this book offends.

This is **MY** mind—in need of an all-out cleanse.
Just the agonizin' thought of those memories—
still makes my ass cheeks come to a clench.
Fuckin' *assho*s . . .

Let's not try to pretend.
That you were there—when I needed a friend.

Fuck!
WHERE WERE ANY OF YOU,
WHEN I NEEDED AN ADULT!?

Where were you, when WE needed an adult?

When we were forced into adult acts,
that mirrored a sadistic cult . . .

this book's the final RESULT!

And you probably don't get it.

"rome's bein' so mean to us.
Did you read what he wrote?
I can't believe he said it!"

Y'g'damn right, I'm speakin' the truth . . .
'n I don't fuckin' regret it.

I refuse to regret it.
To my sanity—I'm forever indebted.

I don't owe any of you SHIT!

I SHOULD SUE ALL OF YOU,
FOR EVERYTHIN' THAT'S
HAPPENED TO ME—SINCE

Y'ALL FUCKIN' LET IT.

Because you probably STILL don't fuckin' get it.

There y'go . . .
I finally said it.
You read it.
I meant it.
Now, don't you forget it.

All my life, I just wanted to make you proud.
Yet it was never gon' happen . . .
'n now—"**I**" finally get it.

But that won't change me—as a man.
It can't.
I refuse to let it.

I'M FUCKIN' EVERYTHIN' 'ERE

Before I get to my point,
let's make one thing fuckin' clear . . .

this world that we live in,
really isn't fuckin' fair.

I never would've guessed
that the end was fuckin' near.

Drivin' all the way to that hospital,
nerves made it hard to fuckin' steer.

God, I'm so missin' my baby boy,
who's no longer fuckin' here.

Now, I'm weepin' like a li'l bitch.
Wipin' away tear after fuckin' tear.

When do we catch a break?
It's been a horrible fuckin' year.

What I've got to say is simple.
But, I wanna make sure you fuckin' hear.

So, I'ma say this shit—out loud.
LOUD 'n fuckin' CLEAR . . .

I CAN'T RELATE TO YOU SELF-CENTERED PEOPLE!
And, at this point, I no longer fuckin' care.

Understand that, leaf?
This burden, I'll no longer fuckin' bear.

It never should've been mine—in the first place.
Your high expectations (of me)—you can fuckin' spare.

It's time I speak my mind.
I'll no longer mute—in fuckin' fear.

That bitch across the room,
is the only mutant fuckin' here.

They'd better not say a g'damn word.
Just stand there—'n fuckin' stare.

I've finally gotten used
to their ignorant fuckin' glare.

I don't know what the hell they see in them.
I really don't . . . I fuckin' swear.

POETIC WORD SLAUGHTER

I'm actually surprised—that they showed up.
I thought for sure they'd steer fuckin' clear.

"SO 'n SO" should've caught these hands,
when they called me a "fuckin' queer."

But, in the back of my mind,
is the reason why we're fuckin' here.

And YOU were jokin' 'bout dancin' an "Irish jig" . . .
at my son's funeral . . . how could you fuckin' dare!?

Along with that delusional leaf of yours.
You two make quite the fuckin' pair.

That bitch could've sent a sugar-coated
Internet message—a fuckin' éclair.

'Cause had they sent me a "Dear rome,"
that shit I'd fuckin' tear.

We didn't need their bullshit speech.
Myself, nor my fuckin' peer.

Yet, time after a millionth g'damn time . . .
it's my patience y'all try to fuckin' wear.

Even though I'm down, 'n out.
I'll always find a way—to fuckin' persevere.

When it comes to integrity, 'n heart . . .
NONE of y'all could ever fuckin' compare!

Not to mine . . .

that conversation can cease right fuckin' here.

As I'm tryin' to mourn my son.
Who's deceased—right over fuckin' there.

Now that THIS "jig" is up . . .
the four of you—can go dance, in a fuckin' square.
Motherfuckers.

WRONG PLACE, WORST TIME

As "SO 'n SO" stood there,
in front of us,
leerin' . . .
the entire tree's,
in the background,
starin'.
The leaves are adamantly
glarin'.
The day (as a whole)
is already exceedingly
overbearin'.

'N they wanna make **THIS**
a thing . . .

the exact drama,
that I'd been stressfully
fearin'.

But . . .
in all honesty . . .
I couldn't even tell you
what "SO 'n SO" was wearin'.

BECAUSE THAT G'DAMN DAY

WASN'T ABOUT THEM!

I don't remember
what was said
between us.

Or, if I even said
anythin' to them—at all.

So, listen up, you
psycho apple,
of a leaf's downfall:
I didn't make that
unwarranted (phone)
call.

I couldn't have cared less,
if they'd even shown up
at all.

**BECAUSE, ONCE AGAIN,
THAT FUCKIN' DAY
WASN'T ABOUT THEM!**

Or them.
Or even about me.

Or ANY combination
of the three.

Or where the fuck
y'all were seated,
so that you could
see (or be seen).

Yes.

You read that accurately.
There was even MORE
family controversy.
About who was seated
frickin' where.

Like I was in
the right state of mind
to even fuckin' care.

Should I have had
to remind you people
why the fuck
you were supposed
t'be there?!

I mean,
SERIOUSLY!?

His mother, 'n I,
are tryin' to grieve.
Our baby boy has just
passed away.

Her family was seated
to her right.
Mine, to the left—on that day.

Yes, she had all of her family
beside her.
While I asked only a seed
to stay.

Which sent most of the
portraits on my tree
into complete, 'n utter,

disarray.

They're all askin'
themselves/each other,
"How does that look, for US?
(About OUR family.)
What does that say?"

It's written all over
each of their faces.
If they were braille,
they'd read "dismay."

Wonderin', why would
rome want it this way?

You did read the previous
pages, right?

Okay . . .

let me bring you
back to the incident,
that preceded this entire
dysfunctional display.

<< rewindin'

□ stopped

▸ press play

Congratulations!
You've done it . . .
you've finally pushed me
over the edge.

For thirty-nine years,
I'd kept my feet
firmly planted . . .
on that ledge.

"I'll maintain my composure.
I won't lose it.
I promise you!" was my self-pledge.

But they crossed the fuckin' line,
on the day that they chose to try
to remove THAT family wedge
at my seed's expense.

At the funeral home . . .
at the services,
for my departed son?

Really!?
REALLY!?

They walked past the altar,
'n grabbed us
each—by a shoulder.

"SO 'n SO came!" they stated

I know who they're referrin' to.
I'm just wonderin'
what type of bullshit
they've been sold. Err . . .
they're not their usual self.
In fact, they're actin' so much bolder.

At the same time I'm wishin'
that the immediate response

(towards their sudden outburst)
had been a li'l more colder.

"SO 'n SO only shows up
to weddings, 'n funerals.
The next time we see them,
might be at yours,"

is what I wish they'd coldly been told. *Brrr . . .*

Yet, I remain respectful,
since they're so much older.

They continued:
"This was meant to bring
you back together!"

"That baby died
for a reason!"

(Now, if my eyes were a gun,
followin' that statement,
you could've called it
"elderly open season."
I'm not a violent person,
but I've become beyond livid
with their personal treason.)

"SO 'n SO showed up!"

HOLD UP

There it is . . .
there's their fuckin' reason.

At this point I'm thinkin' about

pattin' them on their forehead,
'n sayin',

"Well aren't you just a special type
of absolute fuckin' crazy!?"

Some of you,
relatives . . .
no, MOTHERFUCKERS . . .
I tell ya.
Y'all never cease to
amaze me.
These are the final services,
for our deceased child,
'n (right now) you're tryin'
to faze me?

Then you corner my fiancée
with the same insensitive bullshit . . .
'n in that attempt,
you disgrace me?

Hellooo, psychooo . . .
WE JUST LOST
OUR G'DAMN BABY!

Y'all came here to see
fuckin' crazy!?

YOU GOT IT!

I'ma show you rome
gone crazy.
FOLLOW ME.

GAME(S) OVER

I've arrived at the family tree,
deep into the crevices
of the woods.

Lookin' straight up,
towards the peak,
on an uplifted root,
is where I stood.

In the middle
of the ancestral forest.
We're quite a ways,
from the hood.

I've reached my wit's end.
But I think
that's understood.

It's time for somethin' crazier
than my shit-filled
livelihood.

So, we're gonna finish this
right where we started,
for the greater good.

All alone with my thoughts.
Talkin' amongst myself.
The way that you'd expect
I would.

It's slightly sideways rainin'.
There's a sudden chill,

in the darkness of the air.

"I can't believe it's come to this . . ."

As I calmly shed—one final tear.
The culmination of everythin'
that I've thought about,
over this tumultuous year,
has led us to this point
right here.

I survived birth,
for a distinct purpose.
A purpose of which
I was previously
unaware.

Now that purpose,
is speakin' directly to me.
It's in my face . . .
I can hear it screamin',
loud 'n clear.

"rome, this shit's got to end.
*'n it ends—**RIGHT FUCKIN' HERE!**"*

I slightly adjust the volume
on my Beats headphones
that are playin'—in my ear.

If my life could have a theme song,
this is the anthem—that I'd blare:

I can feel the tension risin'.
But "In The Air Tonight"
is all I currently hear.

With the music readily bumpin'
in the background,
'n my heart steadily thumpin'
in the dark . . .
I'm no longer thinkin' in fear.

All of the framed portraits
of the relatives
that I've chosen to leave behind
have now turnt their backs on me,
at the same friggin' time,
towards the branches,
to the rear.

cold stare

It's not the first time
that they've done this to me.
I'm used to turnt backs,
'n derrière.

Not a one looks back towards me.
Not a single gesture
of a return glare.

***"THIS IS HOW YOU WANTED IT
TO GO DOWN?***

FINE BY ME!

***IT'S TIME THAT I LET YOU KNOW,
HOW MUCH I FUCKIN' CARE!"***

*"Where's that g'damn axe!?
Get over here . . .
c'mere!"*

Anticipation's consumed my body,
with goosebumps.

My mind can sense—that the end is near.

With both hands now grasped
firmly around the axe,
I take a deep breath
of that cold, brisk air.

THE DRUM SOLO HITS

MY ADRENALINE'S GOT ME
SO PUMPED UP—FOR THIS SHIT!

"I'LL SHOW YOU,
NOT TO FUCK WITH MY WIT!"

I've given you my heart.
I've given you my all.
I've always played my part
I've given you MY EVERYTHIN',
every single fuckin' time you call.

And in return you give me SHIT!
YOU MOTHERFUCKERS DROPPED
THE BALL!

I've been nothin' but respectful, 'n loyal.
I've been the very best rome
that I could possibly be—for y'all.
Holdin' in every bit of the pain,
while standin' nothin' less than tall.

I've humbled myself
time

after time
after time
after time
after unsolicited time.
So that you'd never have to.
I did that, for you ALL!
This time I'ma write you all off,
FOR GOOD,
'n not for a second stress it.
Not one fuckin' bit.

Then I'ma plant a new family tree.
'N start fresh, with those that
were ride-or-die, from the get . . .
for those that stood by
my entire struggle . . .
for those that watched me grow,
as a man . . .
as a whole . . .

as "rome" . . .

'n truly appreciated
every aspect—of it.

But first,
for good measure . . .
on this old tree—I'ma drop trou,
take a piss,
'n a "CRAZY ASS" shit.

Nah, fuck it.
I'll give 'em two shits!

When you've gotta go,
you've gotta go.

I've gotta go.
'N they've, sure as hell, gotta go.
So, let's get on with it!

As I take a wicked swing,
I'm fully engulfed in despair.

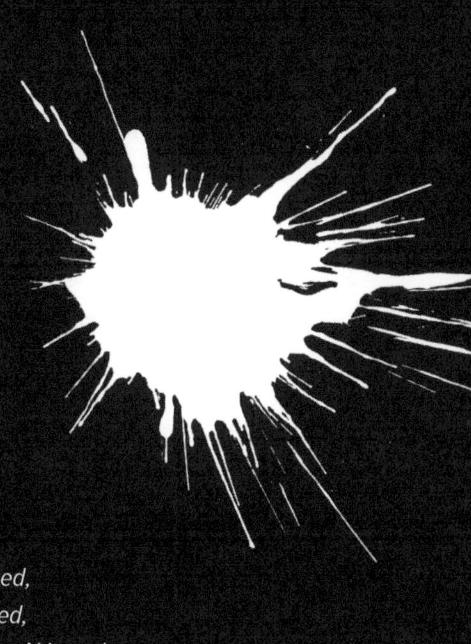

[But a funny thing happens,
when you allow your mind
to finally start thinkin' clear.]

With each chop,
into that large base,
I noticed immediately
that a memory would fade.

I thought to myself,
"Wouldn't it be great,
to forget ALL of those times,
that I've felt betrayed,
all of the games that they've played,
all of the lies that they've conveyed,
all of the poor decisions that we've ALL made.

Better yet:
all of the difficult thoughts,
in these poems,
that I've meticulously parlayed."

Now I'm swingin' vigorously.
I'll no longer be delayed.
Chop, by chop,
in my head,
my memories are replayed . . .

‘n chop, by chop,
from my head,
those same memories
instantaneously fade . . .

. . . the divorce—fade.
. . . the remorse—fade.
. . . the lies—fade.
. . . the cries—fade.
. . . the abuse—fade.
. . . the accuse—fade.
. . . the disrespect—fade.
. . . the neglect—fade.
. . . the disconnect—fade.
. . . the disaffect—fade.
. . . the absurd—fade.
. . . the unheard—fade.
. . . the sadness—fade.
. . . the madness—fade.
. . . the mistrust—fade.
. . . the unjust—fade.
. . . the fears—fade.
. . . the tears—fade.
. . . the rumors—fade.
. . . the humors—fade.

sounds of the tree, as it begins to crack
the portraits simultaneously shake
one by one, NOW they’re lookin’ back
But, it’s already too g’damn late.

I’ve all but tipped over the king,
‘n sealed their ultimate fate.

“HERE’S TO ALL YOUR FUCKED-UP GAMES!”
(I’m just swings away—from declarin’ “checkmate.”)

. . . the pain—fade.
. . . the disdain—fade.
. . . the names—fade.
. . . the games—fade.
. . . the jest—fade.
. . . the obsessed—fade.
. . . the fights—fade.
. . . the plights—fade.
. . . the demise—fade.
. . . the despise—fade.
. . . the rigor—fade.
. . . the vigor—fade.
. . . the scandal—fade.
. . . the vandal—fade.
. . . the cheat—fade.
. . . the indiscreet—fade.
. . . the drama—fade.
. . . the trauma—fade.
. . . the mud—fade.
. . . the blood—fade.

With that final chop,
the tree's gone totally limber.

As I take a quick step backwards,
I exultingly cry out,

"TIMMMM•BERRRR!"

Standin' all alone,
in that forest,
I can tell you . . .
that there was
DEFINITELY a sound.

'Cause I let out a huge

***SIGH**—of relief
as that tall-ass motherfucker
came crashin' down
to the ground.

Throughout my thoughts,
I've written you
a family at odds
(sometimes, at war).
An absolute fuckin' mess!

So, it was aptly fittin',
that my old family tree was tipped
like the king—in a game of chess.

The game, on which I was raised.
Poetic justice . . .
no more, no less.

And I've FINALLY gotten it ALL
off my chest.
For now . . .

Artist: Jason Boucher

ABOUT THE AUTHOR

It has, at one point, been proclaimed that poetry is dead. What better proof that there is a vibrant life of poetry today than the proof found in works of original word-weavers like the Worcester, MA native they call "rome"? His pen leaves traces of gracefulness and the mastery of a magician's hand, all while taking you on a vivid journey through the brightest landscapes and darkest depths of a life you've never lived. That is only a part of the experience provided to you by a poet whose words exceed the traditional notions of poetry, with a unique richness of style and the courage to dive into the unexplored parts of a familiar, yet authentic, human story.

Long-time admirers of the written word might easily find themselves in awe at the proficient wordplay which fills this poetic journey with a flavor of its own, and those who have just been introduced to poetry will remember opening this book as the moment when they entered a completely new, breathtaking world reflecting our deepest fears and desires, failures and victories. Poetry itself is the reflection of a struggle, and rome's words will make you feel the complexity of every step on the path of life, heading into an unknown direction.

One thing is for certain: The path this gifted author took with this release is the one towards eternity, which only the greatest artists have discovered. An eternity of legacy that will guide the strongest and the most vulnerable souls through the chaos we call life. And it will not only teach us the lessons of a life already lived: It will make us laugh, think, cry, fight, smile, dream, and, every single time, it'll help us rise to build a world better than the one we've known.

Moving between the elegance of classical, timeless poetry, and the rawness of urban hip-hop lyricism, between sincerity of love letters and powerful declarations of discontent, anger, and bitterness at the world's miseries, the poetic world of rome conquers even the coldest of hearts. With a distinct approach to rhythmic structures, a natural flow of impeccable rhymes forming into a river of emotions, and an indisputable capacity to transform words into a picturesque representation of a human's most uplifting and most discouraging moments, he shows that form and essence never oppose one another in a complete and well-thought-out work of art.

Nebojša Buhać, Poet/Writer/Musician
Banja Luka, Bosnia and Herzegovina

CREDITS

Author

J.E. rome

Instagram: @poetic.rome

Facebook: @PoeticRome

Twitter: @PoeticRome

Cover Art Sketches

Artist: Jason Boucher

Instagram: @artist_jasonboucher

Cover Art Illustrations

Designer: Cris Cruz

Website: criscruzdesign.com

Reviewers

George Walker Jr.

Amyla Scarcella

Erik Iverson

Tara Erickson

Brian Chenevert

Destinie Curran

Emmanuel Forty

CPSIA information can be obtained
at www.ICGtesting.com
Printed in the USA
BVHW020347230621
610207BV00023B/301